香港特色小吃

DISTINCTIVE SNACKS OF HONG KONG

許陳粉玉編著

萬里機構・飲食天地出版社出版

名家烹飪系列
香港特色小吃

編著者
許陳粉玉

編輯
鄭雅燕

出版
萬里機構・飲食天地出版社
香港鰂魚涌英皇道1065號東達中心1305室
電話：2564 7511　傳真：2565 5539
網址：http://www.wanlibk.com

發行
香港聯合書刊物流有限公司
香港新界大埔汀麗路36號中華商務印刷大廈3字樓
電話：2150 2100　傳真：2407 3062
電郵：info@suplogistics.com.hk

承印
美雅印刷製本有限公司

出版日期
二〇一一年十二月第十八次印刷

ISBN 978-962-14-1518-9

萬里機構 wanlibk.com

「名家烹飪系列」出版説明

飲食是一種文化，烹飪是一門藝術，時至今日，這個看法已得到越來越多人的認同。

中國古書《呂氏春秋》內有「本味篇」，保存了世界上最古老的烹飪理論，提出了一份範圍很廣的食單，記述了商湯時代的天下美食。而被奉為飲食行業的祖師爺，當時的賢相和烹飪名家伊尹在內裏更談到烹飪之道：「鼎足之變，精妙微纖，口弗能言，志弗能喻」。說的是鼎中的變化，精妙而細微，語言難以表達，手裏會做心裏不一定能明白究竟是什麼道理。伊尹指出，這種精妙的技藝，就好像天地之間的陰陽二氣配合得那樣巧妙，又彷彿四季推移一樣，遵循著一定的規律，而有了這種技藝之後，才使佳餚做到久而不腐敗，熟而不過爛，甜而不過頭，酸而不強烈，鹹而不澀嘴，辣而不過度，淡而不寡味，肥而不膩口。

隨著科技的進步和人類知識水平的提高，過往「志弗能喻」的現今都可以找到答案，而要煮出一手好菜式，只要勤學多練，掌握烹飪過程中的竅門，便大有成功的希望。我們看到，有很多享負盛名的烹飪名家，他們之所以能夠成就輝煌，與先天的條件有關，也是本身努力鑽研廚藝，認真探究烹飪學問的結果。為了使更多讀者能分享烹飪之樂和更快地提高廚藝水平，減少彎路，我們特地邀約了香港及世界各地的烹飪名家，用精簡的文字和詳盡的圖片解説來介紹其拿手食譜；至於材料的闡釋，製作的竅門，食譜的有關知識和來龍去脈也一一述及，務使讀者能夠在最短的時間內吸取名家的經驗，把自己的廚藝水平提升到新的境界。

出版「名家烹飪系列」這套叢書是我們的新嘗試，歡迎讀者多提意見，這不啻是本叢書出版得更好的重要依歸。

「名家烹飪系列」編輯委員會

前　言

本書作者與學生合照

「小吃」又稱小食，是正餐以外的食品，與一般佐膳的菜式比較，有份量較少、取材廣泛、食用方便和經濟實惠的特色。

見諸文字記載的小吃品種，其實可以上溯到三千年前，不過「小吃」這個詞，還是在宋朝時才出現，當時有一本名為《能改齋漫錄》的書，裏面便有「世俗例，以早晨小吃為點心」之句。發展至今，小吃已經不止作為果腹的食料，更能提供藝術欣賞和美的享受哩！

小吃的產生和流行，有一定的文化背景和歷史條件，所以中國各地的小食都各具特色，例如北方小食以麵食為主，南方則多以米為基本原料，而具有嶺南風味的廣東小吃，卻以花色繁多，做工精細而馳名。特別在昔日有「食在廣州」之稱的羊城，小食種類尤其豐富多彩，就以豬腸粉為例，原是六十年前廣州流動攤販上街叫賣的大眾小吃，後來則發展到茶樓酒家都有供應，品種也從齋腸到蝦腸、牛肉腸、叉燒腸等，配料和調料也極其講究。

香港的飲食師承自廣州，但「青出於藍而勝於藍」，如今更享有「食在香港」的美譽。香港中西文化交匯，在小吃製作上糅合了華洋特色的用料和製作手法，吃來更令人感到可喜。

香港的特色小吃可分做兩大類：一類是民間節令小吃，這些小吃通常是在家裏製作，用以應節的。因為以前的婦女大多不用上班，所以就有較多時間來做些小吃給家人、鄰居和親友品嚐。如：蘿蔔糕、八寶糯米飯、豬腳薑蛋醋、茶泡等，都是主婦們於節令期間製作的小吃。另一類是街頭小吃，這類小吃通常都是由小販挑著擔子，又或推著車子在街上聚集販賣，好像雞蛋仔、花生米通、白糖糕、砵仔糕、豬皮蘿蔔、碗仔翅等。

隨著時代的演變，現今許多街頭小食都搖身一變成為茶樓酒家中的奉客佳品了。

不過，不少人都感到，在市面上吃到的許多小食不是人工色素過多，就是味精太重，吃後總覺得口裡乾巴巴的，用料和製作過程也沒有什麼標準，要吃到好味和合乎衛生的小吃，似乎越來越難了。有見及此，我編寫了這八十個美味而保健的小吃食譜以饗同好，好讓各位不用「偷師」也能把這些精采的小吃搬到家裏去。

有人說：「美食是很厲害的武器。」但我更認為，「美食之中的小吃是更厲害的武器。」因為無論大小朋友，都會吃得津津有味。說到製作方法，小吃也很「平易近人」，與烹製一般家庭菜式相比，小吃不需應用太多的材料配搭及太複雜的製作技巧，一般只要多試做幾次，便不難成為這方面的「師傅」。況且通過親手製作小食，不但可以作為初入廚者學習廚藝的第一步，更可促成一家大小共享天倫之樂哩！既然如此，不妨就利用餘暇，坐言起行，炮製出糅合你的心意的香港特色小吃來！如果各位讀者在製作時碰上什麼疑難問題，歡迎傳真給我（傳真號碼 26484732），我會盡力解答。

許陳粉玉

Preface

Chinese snacks offer to people, in addition to the staple meal of the day, a very large variety of mini-items of food made available readily and at only commonplace costs. The term made its first appearance in publications of the Sung Dynasty (960-1279A.D.) but the history of the Chinese snacks in fact dates back to well over 3000 years ago. Today, these food specialties are not only the pursuit of city gourmets but are also regarded as a contemporary cooking art.

Chinese snacks of different geographical regions tend to reflect their cultural and historical characteristics. Snacks of North China are mainly noodles and pasta, whereas rice-derived items prevail in South China. Guangdong Province, which lies south of Nanling Range, is well known for the rich variety and the delicacy of its snacks, hence went the saying "Ideal Eating Out in Guangzhou" (Guangzhou being the Provincial capital of Guangdong). The Steamed Rice Sheet Roll is a typical southern snack. Now offered in restaurants with the vegetarian, beef, shrimp and roast pork as its popular varieties, it actually originated from hawker stalls in the streets of Guangzhou about sixty years ago.

Although Hong Kong inherits her cuisine from Guangzhou, the meeting of the Eastern and Western cultures here has led to much improvement on the preparation and serving of the traditional snacks. It is why the city has already succeeded the title of Guangzhou to achieve "Ideal Eating Out in Hong Kong".

Generally speaking, there are two kinds of snacks. The festive foods are made and served at home by housewives for season's celebrities with family members, relatives and friends. Examples are the Turnip Puddings, Eight Treasures Rice Pudding, Assorted Pickles and the New Year Crispy.

The other kind is the hawker snacks. It carries a street culture. Cooked foods are tendered by the mobile hawkers include the Chinese Egg Puff, Peanut Rice Crispy, White Sugar Sponge, Clay-pot Puddings, Soya Pig's Skin and Turnips, "Shark's Fin" Soup made from mung bean thread and many others. It is interesting to note that many of these snacks have now already got a firm place in restaurant menus.

Chinese snacks have by all means been a part of our daily lives. However, modern people are more increasingly aware of the overuse of colourants and other food additives in restaurant foods. Nor are the ingredients and preparation procedure anyhow standardized. I have endeavoured to recommend these 80 recipes to all that intend to make and enjoy their own health-and-environmental-friendly Chinese snacks at home.

Indeed, if regular dishes of Chinese cuisine are fascinating, then, its snacks are even more so. The latter usually involve simpler kitchen work and ingredients, appeal to people of different age groups. Try out Chinese Snacks may well be your first step towards professional cooking. Before long, you may become a cookery expert!

Becky Hui

目錄

Contents

懷舊小食

SELECTIVE OLDIES

CHINESE EGG PUFF

份量：3底
製作時間：45分鐘
To make: 3 pieces
Work Time: 45 minutes

雞蛋仔

◆ **材料：**

麵粉4安士(100克)，生粉1安士(25克)，發粉1平茶匙，雞蛋2隻，沙糖4安士(100克)，淡奶2安士(60毫升)，清水4安士(125毫升)。

◆ **製法：**

1. 將麵粉、生粉及發粉篩勻候用。
2. 用木匙將雞蛋及沙糖拌勻，逐少加入淡奶及清水，拌勻後分次加入粉料中，不停攪拌成稀滑麵漿，不可起粒。
3. 將雞蛋仔模型底面兩面燒熱，掃油後注入粉漿至八分滿，蓋上蓋，將模夾緊，反轉，再置爐上，用中火底面各燒1－2分鐘至雞蛋仔離模及熟透。
4. 用叉將雞蛋仔挑出，趁熱進食。

● **心得：**

新購回來之模型清洗乾淨後燒熱，然後按以上製法做出雞蛋仔。雞蛋仔取出後棄之不要，重複二至三次，直至雞蛋仔較易鬆離為止。

◆ **Ingredients:**

4 oz (100g) plain flour
1 oz (25g) tapioca starch
1 level teaspoon baking powder
2 eggs
4 oz (100g) castor sugar
2 oz (60ml) evaporated milk
4 oz (125ml) water

◆ **Method:**

1. Sieve plain flour, tapioca starch and baking powder together.
2. Beat egg and sugar well with a wooden spoon, gradually mix in milk and water, pour into sieved ingredients, mix to a smooth, lump-free batter.
3. Heat the egg puff mould on both sides, grease it and pour in batter to 80% full, cover, grip and turn the mould upside down, cook over medium heat for 1-2 minutes on each side until set.
4. Unmould egg puff with a fork, serve immediately.

● **Practical Tip:**

To treat a new iron mould, heat and grease after cleaning, prepare the batter, try 2-3 fries, discard egg puffs. Repeat until mould becomes smooth and egg puffs no longer stick.

PEARL CRYSTAL CAKES

份量：20件
製作時間：30分鐘
To make: 20 pieces
Work Time: 30 minutes

水晶西米餅

◆ **材料：**

西米4安士(100克)，馬蹄粉2安士(50克)，沙糖2安士(50克)，清水3安士(75毫升)，豆沙2安士(50克)，油½湯匙。

◆ **製法：**

1. 西米置深碗內，加入浸過西米面的滾水，加蓋浸焗1小時，置筲箕內沖水以去黏性，瀝乾候用。
2. 馬蹄粉加清水浸片刻，過濾入西米中，加糖及油拌勻。
3. 搽模掃一層油，加入1湯匙西米漿，放入豆沙一小粒，再蓋上1湯匙西米漿；用大火蒸約8－10分鐘至西米呈透明狀。
4. 離火，靜候片刻，挑出西米餅供食。

● **心得：**

西米須用大量滾水浸焗透徹，並間中攪拌，以免黏作一團。較大粒的西米可中途再換滾水浸焗。使用前將西米沖水瀝乾即可。

◆ **Ingredients:**

4 oz (100g) sago
2 oz (50g) waterchestnut flour
2 oz (50g) castor sugar
3 oz (75ml) water
2 oz (50g) red bean paste
½ tablespoon oil

◆ **Method:**

1. Pour sufficient boiling water in a deep bowl of sago, cover and soak for 1 hour. Drain in colander, rinse under tap water, drain well.
2. Soak waterchestnut flour in water for a while, sift into sago and mix in sugar and oil.
3. Grease tart moulds, add a tablespoonful of sago mixture, put into a small lump of red bean paste in each mould, top with another tablespoonful of sago mixture. Steam over high heat in 8-10 minutes or until sago turns to transparent.
4. Let cool, unmould and serve.

● **Practical Tip:**

Sago should be soaked in boiling water, stir occasionally to prevent sticky. For larger grains, soak into another bowl of boiling water after half an hour. Rinse and drain well before use.

MINI SUGARY DUMPLINGS

份量：20件
製作時間：20分鐘
To make: 20 dumplings
Work Time: 20 minutes

糖不甩

◆ **材料：**

糯米粉10安士(275克)，暖水1½杯，壓碎烘脆花生4安士(100克)，沙糖3安士(75克)。

◆ **糖水材料：**

片糖4安士(100克)，水½杯。

◆ **製法：**

1. 將½杯水煮滾，加入片糖煮成糖水。
2. 糯米粉用適量暖水開勻，搓成一軟粉糰，再分搓成若干小粒，置大滾水內煮至浮起；將小粒撈起，再放入糖水內，慢火煮片刻，隔去糖水置碟上。
3. 趁熱灑上花生碎及沙糖，即可供吃。

● **心得：**

或可將整件搓好的粉糰用大火隔水蒸至透明及熟透，再置煲內保溫，食時才因應所需份量剪成小塊，趁熱灑上沙糖及花生碎。

◆ **Ingredients:**

10 oz (275g) glutinous rice flour
1½ cup warm water
4 oz (100g) roasted peanuts, crushed
3 oz (75g) castor sugar

◆ **Syrup Ingredients:**

4 oz (100g) slab sugar
½ cup water

◆ **Method:**

1. Bring ½ cup of water to a boil, add in the slab sugar to make the syrup.
2. Add sufficient warm water to glutinous rice flour, mix and knead to a soft dough, roll and divide into small portions, shape into mini dumplings, cook in fast-boiling water till floating on top. Remove and put into syrup, simmer for a short while, drain and dish.
3. Sprinkle crushes peanuts and castor sugar on top of hot sugary dumplings to serve.

● **Practical Tip:**

The dough can be steamed over high heat until cooked. Keep warm in steamer. To serve, cut into small pieces and coat with castor sugar and crushed peanuts.

份量：20粒
製作時間：20分鐘
To make: 20 dumplings
Work Time: 20 minutes

糯米糍

◆ **材料：**

糯米粉10安士(275克)，暖水1½杯，豆沙5安士(150克)，椰茸1杯。

◆ **製法：**

1. 糯米粉與暖水拌勻，搓成柔軟粉糰，分成20等份。
2. 豆沙搓長，切成20小粒。
3. 每份粉糰搓圓按扁，包入豆沙一粒，收口搓圓，放入大滾水內煮至浮起。
4. 瀝乾水分趁熱沾上椰茸，即可食用。

● **心得：**

糯米粉較其他粉類受水，粉糰放久了很易變乾，未使用時最好用濕布或保鮮紙蓋好。包餡時，如發現糯米糰開始乾裂，可將手稍為沾濕重搓即可。

◆ **Ingredients:**

10 oz (275g) glutinous rice flour
1½ cup warm water
5 oz (150g) red bean paste
1 cup desiccated coconut

◆ **Method:**

1. Mix glutinous rice flour with warm water and knead to a soft dough. Divide into 20 equal portions.
2. Knead red bean paste slightly, divide into 20 small lumps.
3. Shape each piece of dough round, press slightly, wrap in a small lump of red bean paste, seal and shape back to a round. Cook dumplings in a large pot of boiling water until floating.
4. Drain and coat with desiccated coconut immediately. Serve hot.

● **Practical Tip:**

Dough made from glutinous rice flour tends to dry up easily, cover with a damp cloth or cling film when not in use. When dough tends to crack, damp and knead again.

CRYSTAL CAKE

份量：16個
製作時間：20分鐘
To make: 16 pieces
Work Time: 20 minutes

水晶餅

◆ **材料：**

澄麵粉4安士(100克)，生粉1安士(25克)，糖3安士(75克)，豬油2茶匙，滾水1杯，蓮蓉／豆沙4安士(100克)。

◆ **製法：**

1. 將澄麵粉及生粉混合，糖及豬油放滾水內煮溶，立刻沖入粉料中，拌至透明及呈糰狀，加蓋焗片刻。
2. 倒出粉糰，放枱上搓至軟滑，分成16小粒，搓圓按扁成水晶皮。
3. 蓮蓉或豆沙分成16小粒，放在水晶皮上，收口搓圓按扁，放餅模內壓實成形後倒出，置掃上油的碟或蒸籠內，大火蒸7分鐘。
4. 趁熱掃上熟油，即可享用。

● **心得：**

水晶皮擺放太久會變硬，所以必須趁熱使用。

◆ **Ingredients:**

4 oz (100g) ungluten flour
1 oz (25g) tapioca starch
3 oz (75g) castor sugar
2 teaspoons lard
1 cup boiling water
4 oz (100g) red bean paste or lotus seed paste

◆ **Method:**

1. Mix ungluten flour and tapioca starch together. Bring sugar and lard to a boil, pour into flour mixture, stir immediately to cook the mixture and form a lump of dough. Cover for 1-2 minutes.
2. Knead dough until soft and smooth, divide into 16 small lumps, press into round crystal pastries.
3. Divide red bean paste or lotus seed paste into 16 small portions. Wrap into each piece of pastry, seal, shape and flatten. Mould to form patterns. Unmould and steam on a greased plate or a bamboo steamer with high heat for 7 minutes.
4. Brush with cooked oil when still hot to serve.

● **Practical Tip:**

It is better to knead and shape dough when it is still soft and hot.

份量：20小碗
製作時間：30分鐘
To make: 20 pieces
Work Time: 30 minutes

砵仔糕

◆ 材料：

粘米粉4安士（100克），糯米粉½湯匙，澄麵粉2½安士（75克），沙糖（或片糖）4安士（100克），水2杯（500毫升），浸透紅豆3湯匙，油少量，竹籤數枝。

◆ 製法：

1. 紅豆置滾水內用慢火煮透，瀝乾候用。
2. 將粉料篩勻，用½杯（約125毫升）水開勻成稠糊。
3. 將餘下之1½杯水（375毫升）煮滾，加入沙糖或片糖煮溶，趁熱撞入粉漿中，攪成滑粉漿。
4. 砵仔掃油，將粉漿倒入砵仔內至九成滿，加入紅豆，用大火蒸20分鐘後取出，稍候片刻才用竹籤挑出即可。

● 心得：

熱水撞入粉漿時，需不停用木杓攪勻，直至粉漿能"掛杓"，即濃度適中。

◆ Ingredients:

4 oz (100g) rice flour
½ tablespoon glutinous rice flour
2½ oz (75g) ungluten flour
4 oz (100g) castor sugar or slab sugar
2 cups (500ml) water
3 tablespoons soaked red beans
a little oil
a few bamboo skewers

◆ Method:

1. Simmer red beans in sufficient boiling water till soft and tender. Drain.
2. Sieve powdery ingredients, mix in ½ cup (125ml) water to form a thick paste.
3. Boil the remaining 1 ½ cups (375ml) water, add sugar to form syrup, pour into flour mixture, stir well to form a smooth batter.
4. Grease clay-pots, spoon in batter to nearly full, steam over high heat for about 20 minutes or until set. Unmould with bamboo skewers after several minutes. Serve hot.

● Practical Tip:

Keep stirring the flour mixture when pouring in the hot syrup. Consistency should just coat the wooden ladle.

BANANA ROLLS

份量：12件
製作時間：45分鐘
To make: 12 pieces
Work Time: 45 minutes

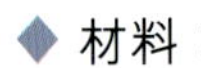

香蕉糕

1. 將糯米粉炒熟成糕粉
Stir-frying the glutinous rice flour to form pudding flour.

2. 糯米粉加糕粉、沙糖、香蕉油及暖水拌勻
Mix all powdery ingredients with banana essence and warm water.

3. 將半份香蕉糕皮蒸熟
Steam half of the prepared dough.

◆ **材料：**

糯米粉5安士（125克），糕粉1½安士（40克），沙糖3安士（75克），暖水約¾杯（200毫升），香蕉油1茶匙，豆沙4安士（100克）。

◆ **撒糕面粉料：**

糕粉1½安士（40克）。

◆ **製法：**

1. 用白鑊將糯米粉炒熟（中火）至呈微金黃色即成糕粉。
2. 將糯米粉，糕粉及沙糖混合，加入香蕉油及適量暖水搓成軟粉糰，取其中半份用大火蒸15分鐘。
3. 將生熟皮混合，搓至極均勻，放枱上開成1厘米厚之長方塊。
4. 將豆沙置兩層牛油紙中間壓成薄塊，放在糯米皮上，推捲成條狀，置已塗油之碟上蒸20－25分鐘。
5. 取出香蕉糕，趁熱滾上糕粉，待冷片刻，用利刀切件即成。

● **心得：**

生熟皮要趁熱才較易搓勻，否則生熟皮會互不"相食"。

◆ **Ingredients:**

5 oz (125g) glutinous rice flour
1½ oz (40g) pudding flour
3 oz (75g) castor sugar
¾ cup (200ml) warm water
1 teaspoon banana essence
4 oz (100g) red bean paste

◆ **For dredging:**

1½ oz (40g) pudding flour

◆ **Method:**

1. Stir-fry glutinous rice flour in a clean dry wok over medium heat until flour turns a light golden brown. It is the pudding flour.
2. Mix glutinous rice flour, pudding flour and sugar together, add banana essence and sufficient warm water to form a soft dough. Steam half of the dough over high heat for about 15 minutes.
3. Combine the two pieces of dough together by kneading vigorously.
4. Roll into a pastry of 1 cm thickness. Roll red bean paste to a thin sheet in between 2 layers of greaseproof paper, put on top of pastry. Roll and steam on greased plate for 20-25 minutes.
5. Coat banana roll with pudding flour when still hot. Cool and cut into pieces with a sharp knife. Serve.

● **Practical Tip:**

To mix the dough, the steamed dough should be very hot; otherwise, it will not mix with the cold dough easily.

4. 將豆沙壓至最薄
Roll red bean paste to paper thin thickness.

5. 鋪上豆沙，捲起成條
Lie red bean paste on rolled pastry, roll to a long sausage form.

WHITE SUGAR SPONGE

份量：20件
製作時間：1-2天
To make: 20 pieces
Work Time: 1-2 days

白糖糕

◆ 材料：

粘米粉12安士(350克)，澄麵粉4安士(100克)，清水4杯，蛋白½隻，白糖1¼磅(600克)。

◆ 糕種：

溫開水½杯，依士(乾酵母)2茶匙，糖½茶匙，粘米粉½杯。

◆ 製法：

1. 將糕種的依士及糖用溫開水浸至溶解，加入粘米粉½杯拌勻後，用濕毛巾蓋好，置室溫5至6小時，待發起至比原來體積大兩至三倍。
2. 將粘米粉及澄麵粉用清水2杯調勻，靜置至清水與濕粉分隔，將上層之水濾去。
3. 白糖加清水2杯煮溶，加入蛋白拌勻，濾清，逐少倒入粉料中攪勻，蓋密待發數小時。
4. 拌入糕種搓勻，用濕布蓋盤口，靜置12小時候發至呈細泡狀。
5. 將白糖漿傾入已舖蒸糕布之蒸籠內，隔水大火蒸25分鐘。
6. 倒出稍冷片刻，切件即成。

● 心得：

發糕種之時間需視乎天氣而定；冬天寒冷需時較長，8－10小時不等；夏天炎熱，需時較短，6－8小時即可。

◆ Ingredients:

12oz (350g) rice flour
4 oz (100g) ungluten flour
4 cups water
½ egg white
1 ¼ lb. (600g) castor sugar

◆ Yeast Dough:

½ cup warm water
2 teaspoon dry yeast
½ teaspoon castor sugar
½ cup rice flour

◆ Method:

1. Dissolve the dry yeast and ½ teaspoon of sugar in warm water, add ½ cup rice flour and mix to a soft dough. Cover with a wet towel and prove for 5-6 hours until the dough has expanded to 2 to 3 times of its original size.
2. Mix rice flour and ungluten flour with 2 cups of water. Set aside until water is separated from the wet flour mixture, filter water off the surface.
3. Dissolve sugar in 2 cups of water, add egg white, mix well, filter to get clear syrup. Pour syrup into wet flour mixture gradually, stir well, cover and prove the mixture for several hours.
4. Mix in yeast dough, knead slightly. Cover with a wet towel and prove for 12 hours until mixture raised like a bubbling sponge.
5. Line bamboo steamer with a piece of greased muslin, pour in the sugary mixture, steam over high heat for 25 minutes.
6. Cool slightly, cut into pieces and serve.

● Practical Tip:

Time for proving yeast dough varied from season to season: in cold winter, it takes about 8-10 hours; in hot summer, it takes about 6-8 hours to rise.

PEANUT RICE CRISPY

To make: 12 pieces
Work Time: 20 minutes
份量：12件
製作時間：20分鐘

花生米通

◆ 材料：

白色棉花糖8安士(225克)，牛油1安士(25克)，即食卜卜米2杯，熟花生¼杯。

◆ 製法：

1. 牛油與棉花糖用慢火煮溶，加入卜卜米及熟花生。
2. 離火拌勻，迅速倒入長方盒內，壓實，置雪櫃內凍至硬透。
3. 取出米通，切件即成。

● 心得：

先用牛油紙墊好長方盒可使米通較易倒出。牛油紙於超級市場有售。

◆ **Ingredients:**

8 oz (225g) white marshmallow
1 oz (25g) butter
2 cups instant rice crispy
¼ cup roasted peanuts

◆ **Method:**

1. Melt the butter and white marshmallow over low heat, keep stirring to avoid sticking, add in rice crispy and roasted peanuts.
2. Remove from heat, stir well and pour into a loaf tin. Press well, chill in refrigerator until firm to touch.
3. Unmould, cut into pieces and serve.

● **Practical Tip:**

Line the loaf tin or box with greaseproof paper first for easy unmoulding. Greaseproof paper is sold in the supermarket.

BLACK SESAME PUDDING

份量：10件
製作時間：1小時
To make: 10 pieces
Work Time: 1 hour

 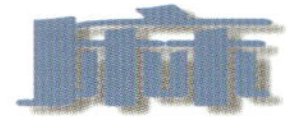 

芝麻糕

芝麻是一種很有益的食品，中醫稱它有補血明目之效。據現代醫學報道，它對慢性神經炎、高血壓等症都有一定的治療作用。記得小時候上茶樓經常可以吃到芝麻糕，但現今卻是「芳蹤杳然」，大概是製作麻煩而利錢不高吧！既然如此，不妨趁假日在家中試製，完成後還可以和剛學會數數目字的小孩子數數它有多少層哩！

1.炒香黑芝麻
Stir-fry black sesame in dry clean wok.

◆ 材料：

黑芝麻1½安士(40克)，沙糖8安士(225克)，水3½杯，粘米粉7安士(200克)，馬蹄粉2安士(50克)，油½湯匙。

◆ 製法：

1. 黑芝麻洗淨吹乾，用白鑊炒香，放攪拌機內，加水6安士(200毫升)攪成芝麻漿，隔去渣滓，候用。
2. 沙糖加水6安士(200毫升)煮成糖水，候用。
3. 用2杯水(500毫升)將粘米粉及馬蹄粉開成粉漿，過濾後加油。
4. 將上列三項材料混合拌勻，倒入方盤內，約½厘米厚，大火蒸三分鐘至凝固。
5. 打開鑊蓋，再傾入第二層芝麻漿，再蒸三分鐘，重複至九層後全底糕再蒸20分鐘。
6. 離火後攤凍，脫模後切件即可。

● 心得：

每次傾入芝麻漿前必須將之調勻，才倒進糕盤內。

◆ Ingredients:

1½ oz (40g) black sesame
8 oz (225g) castor sugar
3½ cups water
7 oz (200g) rice flour
2 oz (50g) waterchestnut flour
½ tablespoon oil

◆ Method:

1. Rinse, drain and air-dry black sesame. Stir-fry in dry clean wok until golden brown. Ground in 6 oz (200ml) water. Put into a sieve to form a fine solution.
2. Dissolve castor sugar in 6 oz (200ml) water.
3. Mix rice flour and waterchestnut flour with 2 cups (500ml) water. Drain and add oil.
4. Add the above three items together, mix well. Pour a thin layer of mixture to about ½ cm thick in a square tin. Steam over high heat for about 3 minutes until set.
5. Remove wok lid, pour in a second layer of mixture, steam for another 3 minutes. Repeat and complete the 9th layer by steaming the whole pudding for 20 minutes.
6. Remove from heat. Cool, unmould, slice and serve.

● Practical Tip:

Mix sesame solution well before steaming.

2.將芝麻漿過濾
Sift ground sesame in a fine sieve.

3.將芝麻漿倒入方盤內，每層蒸3分鐘
Pour mixture into a greased tin, steam each layer for 3 minutes or until set.

WALNUT COOKIES

份量：20個
製作時間：25分鐘
To make: 20 pieces
Work Time: 25 minutes

合桃酥

◆ 材料：

麵粉5安士(150克)，梳打粉¼茶匙，蛋1隻，豬油2½安士(75克)軟黃沙糖3安士(80克)，欖仁1湯匙，蛋黃(塗餅用)1個。

◆ 製法：

1. 預熱焗爐至攝氏200度，焗盤掃油。
2. 麵粉及梳打粉同篩，中間開穴，加入蛋、豬油及軟黃糖，拌勻，搓成光滑粉糰(不宜搓得太久)，分成20小粒。
3. 將每份粉糰搓圓按扁，中間放上欖仁，塗上蛋黃，放焗盤上，入爐焗約15分鐘至金黃色，取出，稍為冷卻即可供吃。

● 心得：

剛出爐之合桃酥較軟身、須待冷才呈鬆脆效果。

◆ Ingredients:

5 oz (150g) plain flour
¼ teaspoon bicarbonate of soda
1 egg
2½ oz (75g) lard
3 oz (80g) soft brown sugar
1 tablespoon olive nuts
1 egg yolk (to glaze)

◆ Method:

1. Preheat oven to 200 °C, grease the baking pan.
2. Sift plain flour and bicarbonate of soda together, make a well in the centre, add egg, lard and soft brown sugar, knead to a smooth dough (do not over knead), divide into 20 small balls.
3. Roll and press each piece of dough, add an olive nut on top, glaze with egg yolk, bake for 15 minutes until golden brown. Remove and cool for a while, serve.

● Practical Tip:

Hot walnut cookies are soft, cool thoroughly to get a crispy result.

“SHARK'S FIN” SOUP

份量：8碗
製作時間：30分鐘
To make: 8 bowls
Work Time: 30 minutes

碗仔翅

◆ **材料：**

粉絲1½安士(40克)，瘦肉3安士(75克)，冬菇5隻，薑1片。

◆ **湯料：**

水4杯，雞粉、糖、鹽、生抽、老抽、麻油各1茶匙。

◆ **芡汁：**

馬蹄粉2湯匙，水4湯匙。

◆ **伴食：**

胡椒粉、浙醋各適量。

◆ **製法：**

1. 粉絲浸軟剪碎，瀝乾。
2. 瘦肉焓熟拆成幼絲；冬菇浸軟切絲。
3. 用1湯匙油起鑊，爆香薑片棄掉；灒酒加入湯料煮滾。
4. 將所有材料加入湯料內，煮滾埋馬蹄粉芡，推稠即可，與胡椒粉及浙醋同上。

● **心得：**

1. 埋芡時要用小火，否則馬蹄粉漿會和粉絲黏作一團。
2. 粉絲當魚翅，乃家喻戶曉之美話。“碗仔翅”乃極受大眾歡迎之街頭小吃，不妨在家裏一試。

◆ **Ingredients:**

1½ oz (40g) mung bean thread
3 oz (75g) lean pork
5 Chinese mushrooms
1 slice ginger

◆ **Ingredients for Soup:**

4 cups water
1 teaspoon chicken powder
1 teaspoon sugar
1 teaspoon salt
1 teaspoon light soya sauce
1 teaspoon dark soya sauce
1 teaspoon sesame oil

◆ **Thickening:**

2 tablespoons waterchestnut flour
4 tablespoons water

◆ **Serve with:**

Pinch of pepper
Pinch of red vinegar

◆ **Method:**

1. Soak mung bean thread until soft. Cut into 1-cm lengths, drain.
2. Boil lean pork until cooked, tear into fine shreds; soak and shred Chinese mushrooms.
3. Heat 1 tablespoon oil in wok, sauté the ginger slice, discard. Sizzle in wine and add ingredients for soup, bring to the boil.
4. Add all shredded ingredients, mix in the thickening when re-boils. Serve hot with pepper and red vinegar.

● **Practical Tips:**

1. Turn down the heat when adding in the thickening; otherwise the waterchestnut flour cooks and turns into lumps easily in high heat.
2. Mung bean thread looks like shark's fin when cooked and the soup is so named. It is a very popular snack in the stalls in Hong Kong Streets. Try it at home today.

SPRING ONION CAKES

份量：4件
製作時間：30分鐘
To make: 4 pieces
Work Time: 30 minutes

葱油餅

◆ 材料：

麵粉5安士(150克)，暖水4安士(125毫升)，鹽1茶匙，油2湯匙，幼葱粒4棵量。

◆ 製法：

1. 麵粉篩至幼滑，加入暖水，攪拌，搓成一幼滑粉糰，分成4份。
2. 枱面灑粉，用木棍將每份粉糰壓成薄方塊。
3. 在麵皮上掃上油一層，灑上適量幼鹽及葱粒。
4. 將兩邊同時捲向中央，覆摺成長條形，略按緊使葱粒不漏出。
5. 將葱油餅開口處向外捲成螺旋形，再用擀麵棍略壓扁。
6. 置中火油鍋內炸至金黃及鬆脆即成。

● 心得：

麵皮壓得越薄，向內捲的層次越多，所炸之葱油餅亦越鬆脆。

◆ Ingredients:

5 oz (150g) plain flour
4 oz (125ml) warm water
1 teaspoon salt
2 tablespoons oil
4 stalks spring onion, diced

◆ Method:

1. Sift plain flour, mix in sufficient warm water, knead to a soft dough. Divide into 4 portions.
2. On a floured pastry board, roll each piece of dough into a paper-thin square.
3. Brush pastry with oil, sprinkle on salt and diced spring onion.
4. Roll from two sides to the centre. Fold to form a long strip. Press to seal the edge.
5. Coil from folded edge to form a round cake. Flatten spring onion cakes slightly.
6. Deep-fry over medium heat until crispy and golden brown. Serve hot.

● Practical Tip:

The thinner the pastry, the more the layers can be, and the fried spring onion cakes will be crispier.

1.在麵皮上掃油，灑鹽及葱粒
Brush pastry with oil, sprinkle on salt and diced spring onion.

2.將麵皮兩端捲向中間，疊成長捲狀
Roll pastry from both sides to centre of pastry.

3.向長條之埋口處捲成螺旋形
Fold and press the open edge to seal, coil from folded edge to form a spiral cake.

4.用擀麵棍將葱油餅略壓平
Flatten spring onion cakes slightly before deep-frying.

STEAMED RICE SHEET ROLLS

份量：8條
製作時間：45分鐘
To make: 8 rolls
Work Time: 45 minutes

豬腸粉

◆ **Ingredients:**

8 oz (225g) long-grain rice
3 cups (750ml) water
1 oz (25g) cornstarch
1 teaspoon salt
1 tablespoon oil
2 tablespoons diced spring onion
3 tablespoons dried shrimps (soaked and diced)

◆ **Soya Sauce:**

2 tablespoons cooked oil
2 tablespoons stock
2 tablespoons light soya sauce
½ tablespoon dark soya sauce
1 teaspoon sugar

◆ **Method:**

1. Soak the long-grain rice for 5-6 hours, add sufficient water and blend to a fine rice solution. Drain well. Add cornstarch, salt and oil, mix with the remaining water.
2. Prepare steamer, line the rack with wet muslin, spoon in a ladle of rice solution, sprinkle on diced spring onion and diced dried shrimps.
3. Cover and steam for 3-5 minutes until set. Take out and turn the rice sheet upside down on a greased smooth surface. Remove the muslin, roll to the shape of a cylinder; cut into sections.
4. Bring the ingredients of soya sauce to boil and pour onto the ricesheet rolls. Serve hot.

● **Practical Tip:**

Special steamers for ricesheet rolls can be bought from shops that sell dim sum equipment. Or a shallow baking tin can be used. Muslin for rice rolls should be well dampened and reused a few times for better result.

◆ **材料：**

粘米8安士(225克)，清水3杯(750毫升)，粟粉1安士(25克)，鹽1茶匙，熟油1湯匙，葱粒2湯匙，蝦米3湯匙，浸軟，粗剁。

◆ **豉油汁：**

熟油2湯匙，上湯2湯匙，生抽2湯匙，老抽½湯匙，糖1茶匙。

◆ **製法：**

1. 粘米洗淨浸5－6小時，加適量水分置攪拌機內磨成米漿，隔去粗粒，加入粟粉，鹽及熟油，與剩餘之水分拌勻。
2. 腸粉鍋內燒熱大半鍋水，架上舖上濕薄布一塊，傾入米漿一湯杓，灑下葱粒及蝦米碎。
3. 加蓋蒸3－5分鐘，取出反轉粉皮於已塗油的平面上，拉起薄布，捲成腸粉，切件上碟。
4. 煮滾豉油汁料，淋上腸粉面，趁熱享用。

● **心得：**

腸粉鍋可到專門售點心用具之店舖購買，或可用淺平方焗盤代替鐵架。腸粉布必須濕透及多用數次，粉皮才易脱離。

CONGEE WITH ASSORTED FISH

份量：6碗
製作時間：1小時30分鐘
To make: 6 bowls
Work Time: 1 hour 30 minutes

◆ 材料：

米3安士(75克)，水8杯，鹽1茶匙，水發魷魚4安士(100克)，炸魚片3安士(75克)，水發豬皮3安士(75克)，胡椒粉、鹽、糖各少許。

◆ 伴食：

適量葱粒及炸花生。

◆ 製法：

1. 將水發魷魚、炸魚片及水發豬皮切絲。
2. 將米洗淨，加鹽1茶匙略醃，加水8杯煮滾，收慢火煮1½小時。
3. 魷魚及豬皮絲放滾水內洗淨，瀝乾，與炸魚片絲一同放入煲好之白粥內，加胡椒粉、鹽、糖各少許，拌勻。
4. 灑上葱粒及花生即可供吃。

● 心得：

水發魷魚及豬皮一般在凍肉公司及豆腐店有售。切絲後要用熱水沖去鹼水味才可使用。

◆ **Ingredients:**

3 oz (75g) rice
8 cups water
1 teaspoon salt
4 oz (100g) blanched cuttlefish
3 oz (75g) fried fish cube
3 oz (75g) blanched pig's skin
Shakes of pepper
Pinch of salt and sugar

◆ **To serve:**

Pinch of diced spring onion and roasted peanuts

◆ **Method:**

1. Shred the blanched cuttlefish, fried fish cube and blanched pig's skin.
2. Rinse and marinate the rice with salt. Add in 8 cups boiling water. Simmer for 1 ½ hours.
3. Rinse shredded cuttlefish and pig's skin in boiling water, drain and add in congee together with shred ingredients. Season with pinch of pepper, salt and sugar. Mix well.
4. Sprinkle diced onion and roasted peanut on top.

● **Practical Tip:**

Blanched cuttlefish and pig's skin are sold in most frozen meat shops and bean curd shops in wet markets. Rinse shredded cuttlefish and pig's skin thoroughly in hot water before use.

CONGEE WITH MINCED BEEF

份量：6碗
製作時間：1小時30分鐘
To make: 6 bowls
Work Time: 1 hour 30 minutes

粉仔牛肉粥

◆ 材料：

米4安士(100克)，鹽1 ½茶匙，水8杯，免治牛肉4安士(100克)，銀絲米粉1安士(25克)。

◆ 調味料：

蛋白2茶匙，水2茶匙，粟粉1茶匙，油1茶匙，鹽¼茶匙，胡椒粉、麻油、油各少許。

◆ 製法：

1. 免治牛肉加調味料拌勻。
2. 米粉剪碎，置滾油內炸鬆，撈起加入免治牛肉，用手黏合，置碗底內。
3. 白米洗淨加鹽略醃，加水煮滾，去泡，收慢火煮1½小時。
4. 將大滾之白粥倒入牛肉碗內，攪至牛肉變熟即可。

● 心得：

1. 炸米粉時可先用少許米粉測試油溫，當米粉置油中便立刻迅速浮起，表示油已夠熱。
2. 撈牛肉及炸米粉時要用手撈，如嫌不夠衛生可用膠手套。若怕牛肉不熟，可將牛肉放入煮好的粥內滾熟，但切忌過火。

◆ **Ingredients:**

4 oz (100g) rice
1½ teaspoon salt
8 cups water
4 oz (100g) minced beef
1 oz (25g) rice vermicelli

◆ **Seasonings:**

2 teaspoons egg white
2 teaspoons water
1 teaspoon cornstarch
1 teaspoon oil
¼ teaspoon salt
Shakes of pepper
Dash of sesame oil

◆ **Method:**

1. Season the minced beef and mix well.
2. Trim rice vermicelli into tiny bits. Sprinkle into a pot of hot oil, dish and drain immediately. Mix with minced beef, leave in deep bowls.
3. Rinse and marinate the rice with salt. Add 8 cups of boiling water, boil and simmer for 1½ hours.
4. Pour boiling congee into beef mixture. Mix and serve when beef turns colour.

● **Practical Tips:**

1. Drop in bit of rice vermicelli to test the readiness of oil. Rice vermicelli should rise and float immediately if the heat is suitable.
2. Traditionally, minced beef is rubbed into the fried rice vermicelli with fingers. To be hygienic, polythene gloves can be used. And to cook beef thoroughly, it can be added into boiling congee, but do not overcook the beef.

節令美食

FESTIVAL SPECIALS

COCONUT ROSETTES

份量：80件
製作時間：1小時
To make: 80 pieces
Work Time: 1 hour

椰汁糖環

◆ **Ingredients:**

1 cup plain flour
1 cup cornstarch
1 cup castor sugar
4 eggs
¾ cup coconut milk
½ cup evaporated milk
1 cup water
Oil for deep-frying

◆ **Method:**

1. Sift plain flour, cornstarch and sugar in a deep bowl, make a well in the centre, drop in eggs, gradually pour in coconut milk, evaporated milk and water to form a thin, smooth batter; stand aside for a while.
2. Heat some oil, put in the rosette mould to heat for a few minutes. Dip the heated mould in batter just to the depth of the mould.
3. Transfer the mould into hot oil, hold until the coated batter coagulates and separates from the mould.
4. Drain the coconut rosettes when it turns to golden brown in colour. Cool, store and serve at anytime.

● **Practical Tip:**

Heat the rosette mould just hot enough to coat the batter and not to cook the batter. Lift the heated mould, hold for a few seconds to drip excess oil, dip in batter immediately to form a nice coat.

◆ 材料：

麵粉1杯，粟粉1杯，沙糖1杯，雞蛋4隻，椰汁¾杯，淡奶½杯，水1杯，油適量(炸糖環用)。

◆ 製法：

1. 將麵粉、粟粉和糖混合，篩於深碗內，中間開一小穴，打入雞蛋，逐少加入椰汁、淡奶及水，不停攪拌成稀麵漿，靜置片刻。
2. 將油燒熱，放入糖環模加熱數分鐘後，將熱模浸入麵漿內(不可浸過模面)。
3. 立刻將模放入熱油中，炸至麵漿凝固及自模鬆脱，並呈金黃色。
4. 取出糖環，瀝乾油分，待冷後便可入罐，隨時供吃。

● 心得：

糖環模必須燒至熱度適中才放入麵漿內，若模型不夠熱便上不到漿，若過熱，則未放入油，麵漿便已脱模。可將模型燒熱後，提起模型，讓多餘油分滴回鑊中，約數秒後立刻浸入麵漿，麵漿便上得恰到好處。

DUMPLINGS IN THIN SYRUP

份量：20粒
製作時間：20分鐘
To make: 20 balls
Work Time: 20 minutes

甜湯丸

◆ 材料：

糯米粉6安士（175克），澄麵粉1½湯匙，暖水5安士（175毫升），片糖1片（切粒），水4杯，片糖5安士（150克），薑1片。

◆ 製法：

1. 糯米粉與澄麵粉拌勻，加適量暖水搓成柔軟粉糰，分成20小粒，按扁，包入片糖，收口搓圓。
2. 燒熱水，加薑片煮至出味，加片糖煮至糖溶。
3. 湯丸放大滾水內煮至浮起及微脹，撈起放入熱糖水內即可。

● 心得：

片糖不要切得太大粒，否則湯丸熟後，片糖餡會仍未完全溶透。

◆ **Ingredients:**

6 oz (175g) glutinous rice flour
1½ tablespoon ungluten flour
5 oz (175ml) warm water
1 piece slab sugar, cut into cubes
4 cups water
5 oz (150g) slab sugar
1 slice ginger

◆ **Method:**

1. Mix glutinous rice flour and ungluten flour together, add sufficient warm water to form a soft dough, divide into 20 small portions. Wrap in slab sugar, seal and roll into ball shape.
2. Bring water and sliced ginger to the boil, add slab sugar, cook until sugar is dissolved.
3. Cook dumplings in fast boiling water till dumplings float on surface. Drain into hot syrup. Serve.

● **Practical Tip:**

Slab sugar cubes for filling should melt when dumplings are cooked, so the size of sugar cubes should not be too large.

CRISPY EGG BOWS

份量：60-80件
製作時間：40分鐘
To make: 60-80 pieces
Work Time: 40 minutes

甜 蛋 散

春節的應節食品種類很多，要想在家中自行製作，蛋散可以算是最簡單的了。只要懂得摺成蝴蝶結的方法，便幾乎可以肯定「勝算在握」。即使家中的小孩子年紀太小，掌握不到製作的竅訣，但給他們一些麵糰，讓他們發揮創意，搓成什麼小豬、飛機、英文字母等各種不同的形狀，全都一併放在鍋裏，炸好後取出齊來分享，也是很好的親子活動。

1.將粉料用蛋和水拌成粉糰
Combine all powdery ingredients with egg and sufficient water.

◆ **材料：**
高筋粉6安士(175克)，發粉¼茶匙，梳打粉⅛茶匙，鹽⅛茶匙，沙糖1湯匙，蛋1隻，水約3安士(80毫升)。

◆ **蘸料：**
糖膠適量。

◆ **製法：**
1. 將粉料篩好拌勻，加入雞蛋及適量清水，開成粉糰，靜置15分鐘。
2. 按板上灑上少許粉料，放上粉糰，用木棍輾成長方塊，切成2.5厘米(1英寸)闊長條，再分切成小方塊。
3. 將每兩塊皮疊起，中間𠝹一切口，將一端自開口處穿過，反轉成蝴蝶結。
4. 用中火將蛋散炸至鬆脆及呈金黃色，食時淋上少許糖膠。

● **心得：**
若不喜吃甜點，將材料稍加變化，便可成為鹹蛋散。只要在皮料中加入1茶匙五香粉，2湯匙黑芝麻，2湯匙南乳汁，不加入沙糖，再用蛋及水開成皮料便可。

2.將粉皮壓薄，切成小方塊，中間𠝹一切口
Roll the pastry thin to an oblong, trim into rectangular pieces and make slits in the centre.

◆ **Ingredients:**
6 oz (175g) high gluten flour
¼ teaspoon baking powder
⅛ teaspoon bicarbaonate of soda
⅛ teaspoon salt
1 tablespoon castor sugar
1 egg
3 oz (80ml) water

◆ **To Serve:**
Adequate amount of golden syrup

◆ **Method:**
1. Sieve all powdery ingredients together. Add in the beaten egg and water to form soft dough. Set it aside for about 15 minutes.
2. Sprinkle some flour on the pastry board, roll the dough into a thin sheet, trim and cut into 2.5cm (1-inch) wide strips, then divide them into small rectangles.
3. Put 2 pieces of pastries together, dampen and make sharp slit in the centre, pull one end through the open slit as a bow shape.
4. Deep-fry in medium hot oil till the egg bows become crispy and turn to golden brown in colour. Serve with the golden syrup.

● **Practical Tip:**
You can make Savoury Egg Bows other than this sweet taste of snack. Add 1 teaspoon of five-spice powder, 2 tablespoons each of black sesame and juice from fermented red bean curd into the powdery ingredients (except sugar), mix with egg and water.

3.將兩塊小麵塊疊起，自開口處反轉麵塊，摺成蝴蝶結
Dampen each piece of pastries slightly, put another piece on top, turn one end through the slit, fold to form a bow shape.

份量：40－50個
製作時間：1小時
To make: 40-50 dumplings
Work Time: 1 hour

油角仔

◆ **材料：**

(1) **皮料**：麵粉8安士（225克），豬油粒1安士（25克），油1安士（25克），沙糖2安士（50克），蛋汁3安士（75毫升）。

(2) **餡料**：炒香白芝麻2安士（50克），壓碎熟花生2安士（50克），砂糖3安士（75克）。

◆ **製法：**

1. 將6安士（175克）麵粉過篩，加入豬油粒用手指搓入麵粉中至極幼細，加入沙糖，拌勻，逐少加入生油及蛋汁，拌勻，逐少撥入餘下之2安士（50克）麵粉，輕搓成一不黏手之粉糰。
2. 將餡用料混合，待用。
3. 枱上灑上乾麵粉，用棍將麵皮輾至1分厚，用圓玻璃杯口鈒成小圓塊。
4. 包入適量餡料，對摺成半月形，收口鎖邊，用中火油炸透，瀝乾油分，待冷即可入罐，隨時享用。

● **心得：**

包角仔時，皮的邊緣盡量不要沾有糖餡，否則落油時角仔會很易爆開的。

◆ **Ingredients:**

(1) **Dough:**
8 oz (225g) plain flour
1 oz (25g) diced lard
1 oz (25g) oil
2 oz (50g) castor sugar
3 oz (75ml) beaten egg

(2) **Filling:**
2 oz (50g) fried white sesame
2 oz (50g) crushed roasted peanuts
3 oz (75g) castor sugar

◆ **Method:**

1. Sieve 6 oz (175g) of the plain flour, rub in lard, add sugar, bind with oil and beaten egg, mix well. Gradually add in remaining flour, slightly knead to form a soft dough.
2. Mix ingredients for filling. Set aside.
3. Sprinkle some flour on the table. Roll the pastry to about ¼ cm thick. Cut into small rounds with a glass or plain cutter.
4. Wrap in sufficient filling on each piece of pastry, half-fold, press rim to seal dumplings, pinch to form patterns on curve side. Deep-fry the dumplings till crispy and golden brown in colour. Drain, cool and store.

● **Practical Tip:**

Keep rim of pastry rounds free from sugary filling or dumplings will crack in oil when deep-frying.

份量：24個
製作時間：30分鐘
To make: 24 doughnuts
Work Time: 30 minutes

笑口棗

◆ 材料：

麵粉6安士(175克)，發粉2茶匙，沙糖3安士(75克)，豬油1湯匙，冷開水約6湯匙，白芝麻1杯。

◆ 製法：

1. 將麵粉及發粉篩匀，加入沙糖及豬油，用適量冷開水拌成一軟滑粉糰，靜置半小時，候用。
2. 將粉糰搓長，切成24小粒，將之搓圓，掃濕後再沾上一層白芝麻，搓圓。
3. 燒油至七成熱，離火，放入笑口棗，炸至浮面後開中火，炸至笑口棗爆裂及呈金黃色，盛起，瀝乾油分，待冷即可入罐。

● 心得：

離火放入笑口棗，可免芝麻煮得過火及可將笑口棗炸透；但不要太遲回火，否則笑口棗會吸油過多而變得肥膩。炸時要經常使用鑊鏟或炸籬轉動笑口棗。

◆ **Ingredients:**

6 oz (175g) plain flour
2 teaspoons baking powder
3 oz (75g) castor sugar
1 tablespoon lard
6 tablespoons (approximately) cold water
1 cup white sesame

◆ **Method:**

1. Sieve plain flour and baking powder together, add sugar and lard, mix in sufficient cold water to form a soft dough, set aside for half an hour before use.
2. Roll and divide dough into 24 small pieces, roll each piece of dough to a ball shape, damp with water, coat evenly with white sesame, shape well.
3. Heat oil until hot, turn off the heat, slide in doughnuts, return to heat when doughnuts start to float, deep-fry over medium heat until the doughnuts burst and turn to golden brown in colour, drain, cool and store.

● **Practical Tip:**

Turning off the heat before sliding in the doughnuts can avoid sesame coating from over-burning. Cold oil tends to penetrate into doughnuts, so return to heat when doughnuts start to burst and keep turning the doughnuts with a ladle all the time.

SESAME DUMPLINGS

份量：20個
製作時間：30分鐘
To make: 20 dumplings
Work Time: 30 minutes

煎堆仔

◆ **材料：**

糯米粉10安士（275克），水1½杯，片糖5安士（125克），白芝麻1杯。

◆ **製法：**

1. 片糖加水煮溶，攤至稍暖，加入糯米粉攪拌成團，搓軟，分成20小粒，搓圓。
2. 掌心濕水，將糯米粉糰略搓，沾上白芝麻，搓圓。
3. 將油燒至七成熱，離火，放入煎堆，炸至略浮，開火，用平杓略壓煎堆使其逐漸脹大，並呈空心狀。
4. 炸透至皮脆及呈金黃色，瀝乾油分熱食。

● **心得：**

炸煎堆宜用大鑊油，讓煎堆有空間膨脹。壓煎堆之力要均勻及分次加壓，油溫不宜過猛因芝麻很易上色。

◆ **Ingredients:**

10 oz (275g) glutinous rice flour
1 ½ cups water
5 oz (125g) slab sugar
1 cup white sesame

◆ **Method:**

1. Dissolve slab sugar in 1 ½ cups water. Cool down a bit. Mix with glutinous rice flour and knead to form a soft dough. Roll and divide into 20 small portions.
2. Damp palms a bit, roll each dumpling into a round, coat with white sesame, shape well.
3. Heat oil to 70% hot, turn off the heat, slide in dumplings, turn on the heat again when the dumplings start floating. Press them constantly with a ladle till the dumplings expand and become hollow in shape.
4. Deep-fry until become crispy and turn to golden brown in colour. Drain well and serve hot.

● **Practical Tip:**

Oil used here should be sufficient to allow room for dumplings to expand. Apply pressure gradually when dumplings start to float and expand. Avoid using high heat because white sesame will get burnt easily.

FRIED RED BEAN DUMPLINGS

份量：12個
製作時間：45分鐘
To make: 12 pieces
Work Time: 45 minutes

◆ Ingredients:

10 oz (275g) glutinous rice flour
2 tablespoons ungluten flour
1 ½ cup (375ml) warm water
1 tablespoon castor sugar
8 oz (225g) red bean paste

◆ Method:

1. Sieve glutinous rice flour and ungluten flour together, mix in sufficient warm water to form a soft dough. Halve into two.
2. Put half of the dough on a greased plate and steam for about 10-15 minutes until cooked. Mix steamed dough with the reserved dough, knead with castor sugar at the same time. Divide into 12 portions, press into round pastries.
3. Divide red bean paste into 12 small lumps, wrap each into pastries, shape into triangles, seal edges. Deep-fry until golden brown in colour. Drain well and serve.

● Practical Tip:

The dough is also suitable for making savoury meat dumplings, but fillings should be stir-fried and cooled before use. For a crispier result, knead in a lump of lard to the dough.

◆ 材料：

糯米粉10安士(275克)，澄麵粉2湯匙，暖水1½杯(375毫升)，沙糖1湯匙，豆沙8安士(225克)。

◆ 製法：

1. 糯米粉與澄麵粉篩勻，加入適量暖水開成軟粉糰，分成兩份。
2. 將1份粉糰放在塗了油的碟上，蒸10－15分鐘至熟，趁熱與餘下之生粉糰搓勻，擦入沙糖，搓至極均勻，搓長切成12份，壓成圓塊。
3. 豆沙搓長，分成12小粒，包入糯米皮中，做成三角形，用大火油炸至呈金黃色即可。

● 心得：

此皮料亦可製作鹹水角，但肉餡須預先炒熟，待涼後才用。搓皮時可加入少許豬油使皮更鬆脆。

RICE DUMPLINGS IN BAMBOO LEAVES

份量：8隻
製作時間：3小時
To make: 8 pieces
Work Time: 3 hours

家鄉鹹肉粽

1.將包粽用料預備好
Prepare all ingredients for rice dumplings accordingly.

◆ 材料：

竹葉24塊；水草8條；糯米1¼磅(600克)；綠豆邊6安士(175克)；冬菇8隻；腩肉10安士(275克)；蝦米1½安士(40克)。

◆ 腩肉醃料：

鹽1茶匙，五香粉½茶匙，麻油少許。

◆ 製法：

1. 將竹葉浸透，剪去硬蒂；水草浸透；糯米洗淨後瀝乾，加鹽1茶匙拌勻；綠豆邊浸片刻，洗淨，瀝乾；冬菇浸軟後去蒂；腩肉洗淨，切件後用醃料拌勻待3小時；蝦米浸軟。
2. 將兩塊竹葉重疊，屈摺成一碗形。
3. 底層放一大匙糯米，放上各項餡料，最後加綠豆邊及糯米。
4. 左手將粽兜托好，自前端另加竹葉一塊。
5. 將竹葉尾端豎起，左手將餡料封口，右手將末端竹葉向下屈摺，固定粽形。
6. 用水草將鹹肉粽紮實，置浸過面之滾水內烚2小時，撈起即成。

● 心得：

可適量地加鹹蛋黃，栗子肉，瑤柱等作為餡料。為方便移動或撈起粽子，可用一粗水草將粽子串起才放進滾水內。

◆ Ingredients:

24 bamboo leaves
8 straws
1¼ lbs (600g) glutinous rice
1 teaspoon of salt
6 oz (175g) green split beans
8 Chinese mushrooms
10 oz (275g) pork belly
1½ oz (40g) dried shrimps

◆ Marinade for pork belly:

1 teaspoon salt
½ teaspoon five-spice powder
Dash of sesame oil

◆ Method:

1. Prepare the ingredients accordingly: soak and trim the bamboo leaves; soak the straws thoroughly; rinse and drain the glutinous rice and mix in 1 teaspoon of salt. Rinse and drain the green spilt beans.
2. Hold two pieces of bamboo leaves together and fold to form a leave-shape bowl, hold in position.
3. Spoon in a layer of glutinous rice and green split beans first, add other fillings and finish with a tablespoonful of glutinous rice.
4. Keep holding the dumpling with the left hand, aside in the third piece of bamboo leave in the front.
5. Hold the dumpling upright and wrap with the left hand to seal the opening. Fold the tip part downward and hold the dumpling in position.
6. Tie and fix dumpling in shape with a long straw. Add all wrapped dumplings in a large pot of boiling water, boil for 2 hours. Drain, untie and serve.

● Practical Tip:

Salted egg yolk, chestnut and dried scallops can be added as fillings. Tie all rice dumplings in one thick straw for easy carrying.

2.將兩塊竹葉重疊，屈成碗狀
Hold 2 bamboo leaves together, bend and fold to form a leaf-bowl in one end.

3.放入糯米及餡料
Add a spoonful of glutinous rice and green split beans in bottom, add other fillings and top with another layer of glutinous rice.

4.加第三塊竹葉於前方
Slide in a third piece of bamboo leaf, hold in position.

5.將粽豎起，掃平尾部，左手將粽包好收口
Hold dumpling upright, seal opening on side first.

6.右手將尾部向下屈，固定粽形
Tidy the tip leaves and fold downward to form four sharp corners, grip dumplings firmly.

7.用水草紮好鹹肉粽
Tie and fix dumplings in shape with straws

EIGHT TREASURES RICE PUDDING

份量：4碗
製作時間：1小時15分鐘
To make: 4 bowls
Work Time: 1 hour 15 minutes

八寶糯米飯

◆ 材料：

糯米8安士(225克)，砂糖3安士(75克)，豬油1安士(25克)，豆沙4安士(100克)，提子乾1湯匙，青、紅車厘子(櫻桃)2粒，去核西梅4粒，杏脯肉2粒。

◆ 製法：

1. 將西梅、杏脯肉及青、紅車厘子各切成粒。
2. 糯米洗淨浸過夜，隔水，大火蒸熟，趁熱加入砂糖及豬油拌勻。
3. 飯碗掃油，放入乾什果碎排成圖案，加約4湯匙甜糯米飯，按實，放入少許豆沙，再加甜糯米飯至滿，掃平。
4. 蓋上錫紙隔去倒汗水，大火蒸10－15分鐘。
5. 取出，反轉底向上即成。

● 心得：

蒸糯米飯之時間需1小時或以上，如欠耐性，可用電飯煲煮糯米飯，比例是：2杯糯米用1½杯水，但蒸的糯米飯質感較煮的好。

◆ **Ingredients:**

8 oz (225g) glutinous rice
3 oz (75g) castor sugar
1 oz (25g) lard
4 oz (100g) red bean paste
1 tablespoon raisins
2 red /green glaced cherries
4 pitted prunes
2 preserved apricot

◆ **Method:**

1. Cut prunes, preserved apricots into dices.
2. Rinse and soak glutinous rice overnight, drain and steam over high heat till cooked, mix in castor sugar and lard when still hot.
3. Grease rice bowls, line with diced, dried fruits to form patterns, fill with 4 tablespoons of sweetened glutinous rice, add a small piece of red bean paste in the centre. Top with another layer of rice to fill the bowls. Flatten the top.
4. Cover with foil and steam for 10-15 minutes over high heat.
5. Unmould with underside up. Serve.

● **Practical Tip:**

Steamed glutinous rice takes about 1 hour or more to cook. For convenience, electric rice cooker can be used. Use 1 ½ cups water to 2 cups of rice and cook as usual. Texture of steamed rice is better than boiled one.

份量：5個
製作時間：2小時
To make: 5 pieces
Work Time: 2 hours

雙黃蓮蓉月

◆ 材料：

皮料：麵粉6安士（175克），吉士粉1湯匙，花生油3湯匙，糖膠4湯匙，普洱濃茶1湯匙，鹼水2滴。

餡料：白蓮蓉1½磅（600克），鹹蛋黃10個。

掃皮用：生油、蛋。

◆ 製法：

1. 將皮用料混合，拌成軟粉糰，分成5份，搓圓，候用。
2. 白蓮蓉分成5份，搓圓，中間按孔，包入鹹蛋黃兩個，埋口搓圓。
3. 預熱焗爐至190°C；餅模灑上薄粉一層；焗盤掃油及在案枱上灑粉。
4. 用木棍將麵皮按成圓薄餅皮，包入蓮蓉餡一份，埋口搓圓，放入餅模，壓平，力度要適中。
5. 敲出月餅，用噴水壺將餅略噴濕，放入烘爐先焗10分鐘，取出掃上皮料，再焗30分鐘。
6. 取出月餅再掃一次皮，重焗10－15分鐘至餅呈金黃色為止。
7. 取出待冷透後入罐，存放2－3天回油後即可享用。

心得：

1. 新購之月餅模清洗乾淨後，先用竹籤將餅模旁之小孔通一通及用竹籤塞着小孔，注入生油浸一夜至餅模潤透為止。用吸油紙或油布印去表面油質便可使用。
2. 蓮蓉及皮之大小須依月餅模之大小而確定。如製純蓮蓉月或減少鹹蛋黃，蓮蓉的份量便要增加。

◆ Ingredients:

Dough:

6 oz (175g) plain flour
1 tablespoon custard powder
3 tablespoons peanut oil
4 tablespoons golden syrup
1 tablespoon Chinese dark tea
2 drops alkali water

Filling:

1 ½ lb (600g) lotus seed paste
10 salted egg yolks

To glaze:

Oil mix with beaten egg

◆ Method:

1. Mix ingredients for dough, knead to a smooth dough, divide into 5 portions, shape into ball shapes.
2. Divide lotus seed paste into 5 portions, press and wrap in two salted egg yolks in each portion, seal and shape well.
3. Preheat oven to 190 °C; dust mooncake mould with flour, grease baking sheet and flour pastry board.
4. Roll each piece of dough to a thin round, wrap in a portion of filling. Seal and shape. Put in the prepared mould. Apply pressure evenly.
5. Unmould and arrange on baking sheet, spray slightly with water. Bake for 10 minutes, take out and glaze with oil and beaten egg. Bake for another 30 minutes.
6. Take out cakes and glaze again. Bake for 10-15 minutes until golden brown in colour.
7. Cool and keep in air-tight tins for 2-3 days. Serve when a nice glossy colour is formed.

Practical Tips:

1. To treat a new wooden mould, clean and block the two holes on the sides of mould with toothpicks. Fill mould with oil and soak for overnight until mould is well greased. Wipe with kitchen paper before use.
2. Sizes of filling and pastry should scale to the size of mould. If less salted egg yolk is used, weight of lotus seed paste should be increased.

製作時間：30分鐘

Work Time: 30 minutes

賀年茶泡

◆ **材料：**

花生4安士（100克），芋頭半個，薯仔1個，番薯1個，茨菇4個，腰果4安士（100克），幼鹽適量。

◆ **製法：**

1. 花生浸滾水，去衣，吹乾。
2. 芋頭、薯仔、番薯及茨菇去衣，切成小薄片，用滾鹽水浸片刻，撈起鋪平吹乾。
3. 腰果用鹽水焓片刻，取出吹乾。
4. 將各茶泡料分別放沸油內炸至金黃色，撈起瀝乾油分，趁熱灑上幼鹽，待冷入罐。

● **心得：**

各款茶泡料應獨立下油鑊，不要全部一起炸，因它們的受火程度不同。

◆ **Ingredients:**

4 oz (100g) peanut
½ taro
1 potato
1 sweet potato
4 arrowroot
4 oz (100g) cashew nut
Some salt

◆ **Method:**

1. Soak peanut in boiling water, skin and air-dry.
2. Peel taro, potato, sweet potato and arrowroot, cut into small thin slices, rinse in hot salt solution drain, spread and air-dry.
3. Boil cashew nut in salt water, drain and air-dry.
4. Deep-fry the above ingredients separately in hot oil until golden brown. Drain and dust with salt. Cool and store in air-tight tins.

● **Practical Tip:**

Fry the crispies separately, they brown at different temperature.

製作時間：2小時
Work Time: 2 hours

豬腳薑蛋醋

◆ **材料：**

甜醋4支，酸醋1支，薑2磅(900克)，豬手(斬件)2磅(900克)，蛋(烚熟、去殼)1打，鹽¼湯匙。

◆ **製法：**

1. 用慢火將甜醋燒滾。
2. 薑去皮洗淨，吸乾水分，拍鬆，用白鑊炒乾使去多餘水分，灑入幼鹽炒片刻，盛起加入甜醋內慢火煲1小時。
3. 豬手洗淨，放大滾水內滾數分鐘使去羶味，盛起過冷，用布吸乾水分。
4. 將1支酸醋加入薑醋內，翻滾後加入豬手，慢火煲半小時，離火，待冷即可貯存。

● **心得：**

薑醋若需久存，薑及豬手放入時必須吸至極乾，否則多餘之水分會令薑醋易變壞；煲蓋之倒汗水也易使薑醋變質，所以煲薑醋之器皿宜用瓦煲。雞蛋適宜於2天前才加入薑醋內滾10－15分鐘後離火，1－2天後加熱進食，質感適中不會過實。

◆ **Ingredients:**

4 bottles black sweetened vinegar
1 bottle black rice vinegar
2 lbs. (900g) ginger
2 lbs. (900g) pig's trotters
1 dozen hard-boiled eggs
¼ tablespoon salt

◆ **Method:**

1. Heat sweetened vinegar slowly until boils.
2. Skin, dry and crush ginger, stir in dry heated wok to dry thoroughly, sprinkle in salt, keep stirring for a while, dish and add into sweetened vinegar, simmer for 1 hour.
3. Blanch pig's trotters in boiling water for a few minutes, rinse and towel-dry.
4. Add rice vinegar to ginger pickles, when boils, add trotters and simmer for ½ hour. Cool and store.

● **Practical Tip:**

Water vapour will affect the storage life of pickles, all ingredients should be well-dried before added into vinegar. To prevent condensed water vapour, clay pots are of good choice. For best texture, add hard-boiled eggs (re-boil for 10-15 minutes) 2 days before serving.

TURNIP PUDDINGS

份量：2底
製作時間：1小時30分鐘
To make: 2 pudding tins
Work Time: 1 hour 30 minutes

蘿蔔糕

◆ **Ingredients:**

4 lbs. (1.5kg) turnips
1 lb. (450g) rice flour
3 oz (75g) ungluten flour
8 Chinese mushrooms
2 oz (50g) dried shrimps
6 oz (175g) Chinese sausage and preserved pork
6 cups water

◆ **Seasonings:**

3 teaspoons salt
2 teaspoons sugar
Dash of sesame oil
Shakes of pepper

◆ **Garnish:**

Dash of diced parsley, spring onion and roasted white sesame

◆ **Method:**

1. Soak and dice the Chinese mushrooms. Clean and soak the dried shrimps. Blanch and steam the Chinese sausage and preserved pork; dice.
2. Sieve rice flour and ungluten flour together into a large bowl, add seasonings, 3 cups of water to form a batter.
3. Sauté diced ingredients in oil, sizzle in wine, stir well, Dish.
4. Peel and grate turnips into long shreds, sauté with a little oil, add 3 cups of boiling water, bring turnips to boil, immediately pour mixture into the batter, stir to obtain a sticky consistency. Add other ingredients, mix well.
5. Pour pudding mixture into a greased tin. Steam over high heat for 1 hour until cooked.
6. Garnish, cool, slice and shallow-fry till it turns to golden brown in colour on both sides.

● **Practical Tip:**

Texture of pudding can be adjusted according to one's desire. For a firmer texture, add a little more rice flour or use less turnips. Choices of assorted meat can be optional.

◆ **材料：**

白蘿蔔4磅(1.5公斤)，粘米粉1磅(450克)，澄麵粉3安士(75克)，冬菇8隻，蝦米2安士(50克)，臘腸、臘肉6安士(175克)，暖水3杯，滾水3杯。

◆ **調味料：**

鹽3茶匙，糖2茶匙，麻油、胡椒粉各少許。

◆ **裝飾：**

芫荽碎、葱粒、炒香白芝麻各少許。

◆ **製法：**

1. 冬菇浸軟，切粒；蝦米洗淨，浸軟；臘腸、臘肉洗淨後出水、蒸熟及切粒。
2. 粘米粉與澄麵粉篩入大碗內，加調味料，用3杯暖水開成粉漿。
3. 冬菇、蝦米、臘肉及臘腸起油鑊，爆香，灒酒，炒勻盛起。
4. 白蘿蔔去衣刨絲，放油鑊略炒，加滾水3杯，煮滾趁熱撞入粉漿內，拌成糊狀，加入其他材料拌勻。
5. 糕盤掃油，倒入糕料，大火蒸1小時或至糕熟。
6. 趁熱灑上白芝麻，芫荽碎及葱粒，待冷切件，用油煎香，趁熱供吃。

● **心得：**

吃蘿蔔糕的口味因人而異，如喜歡較硬的糕底，可加少量粘米粉或減少蘿蔔也可。另外，配料時亦可隨意加減。

滋味甜品

NOURISHING DESSERTS

WALNUT SWEET TEA

份量：10碗
製作時間：30分鐘
To make: 10 bowls
Work Time: 30 minutes

合桃糊

◆ **材料：**

去衣合桃6安士（175克），冰糖8安士（225克），米2湯匙，水5杯，淡奶2安士（50毫升）。

◆ **製法：**

1. 合桃放入淡鹽水焓3分鐘，洗淨瀝乾。待乾透後用慢火油炸至浮起及呈金黃色，取出隔去多餘油分。
2. 白米浸透後放攪拌機內加水少許打成漿狀，過濾成米漿。
3. 用1杯水將合桃打成漿狀，過濾成合桃漿。
4. 將4杯水加冰糖煮溶，加入合桃漿及適量米漿煮至微稠。
5. 加入淡奶，拌勻熱食。

● **心得：**

去衣合桃可到海味店購買，有些雜貨店也有發售。去衣合桃不宜久存，最好置雪櫃內保質。

◆ **Ingredients:**

6 oz (175g) skinned walnuts
8 oz (225g) rock sugar
2 tablespoons rice
5 cups water
2 oz (50ml) evaporated milk

◆ **Method:**

1. Blanch skinned walnuts in salt water for 3 minutes. Drain and air-dry. Deep-fry over medium heat until cooked and brown. Drain.
2. Soak rice and liquidize in an electric blender, filter as rice solution.
3. Ground walnut in 1 cup of water. Filter as walnut solution.
4. Dissolve rock sugar in remaining 4 cups of water, add walnut solution, when boils, thicken with rice solution.
5. Mix in evaporated milk, serve hot.

● **Practical Tip:**

Skinned walnuts can be bought from most Dried Seafood Shops. Keep skinned walnuts in refrigerator for longer shelf life.

份量：8碗
製作時間：20分鐘
To make: 8 bowls
Work Time: 20 minutes

杏仁糊

◆ 材料：

南杏4安士（100克），北杏1湯匙，白米2湯匙，水5杯，冰糖5安士（150克），淡奶2安士（50毫升）。

◆ 製法：

1. 南杏用熱水燙過，去衣，與北杏一起用1杯水浸約1小時，放入攪拌機內打成杏仁漿，過濾候用。
2. 白米用½杯水浸1小時，加入攪拌機內攪成米漿，過濾候用。
3. 用餘下之3½杯水將冰糖煮溶，加入杏仁漿，煮滾，用適量米漿調煮成糊狀，最後加入淡奶，拌勻熱食。

● 心得：

杏仁化痰止咳，潤肺養顏，使皮膚潔白，幼滑。杏仁糊主要成分為連衣大南杏，北杏用多了帶苦澀味，藥性較重。甜度可自行調試，惟杏仁漿及米漿必須用密篩過濾，才達至幼滑之效果。

◆ Ingredients:

4 oz (100g) sweet apricot kernel
1 tablespoon apricot kernel
2 tablespoons rice
5 cups water
5 oz (150g) rock sugar
2 oz (50ml) evaporated milk

◆ Method:

1. Blanch sweet apricot kernel, remove skin, soak in 1 cup of water with apricot kernel for 1 hour, liquidize in an electric blender, filter as almond solution.
2. Rinse and soak rice in ½ cup of water for 1 hour, liquidize and filter as rice solution.
3. Boil the remaining 3½ cups water and dissolve rock sugar, add almond solution, stir until boils, thicken with rice solution, add evaporated milk, serve hot.

● Practical Tip:

Chinese almonds help to remove sputurn and relieve coughs, nourish the lungs, make the skin white and smooth. The Almond Sweet Tea is specially good for ladies. To achieve a smooth and fine result, pass the almond and rice solutions through a fine sieve before use.

PEANUT SWEET TEA

份量：6碗
製作時間：30分鐘
To make: 6 bowls
Work Time: 30 minutes

花　生　糊

◆ **材料：**

珠豆（花生）4安士（100克），水5杯，冰糖5安士（150克），白米2湯匙，淡奶2安士（50毫升）。

◆ **製法：**

1. 珠豆連衣放入150°C之焗爐焗15－20分鐘或至呈金黃色，取出待冷，去衣，放入電攪拌機內，加水1杯，攪成花生漿，隔至幼滑。
2. 白米洗淨用半杯水浸透，連水放入攪拌機內攪成米漿，濾去粗米粒，候用。
3. 將餘下3½杯水煮滾，加入冰糖待溶，加入花生漿，慢火煮片刻（須不停攪拌，以免黏底）。
4. 用適量米漿調煮至花生糊微稠，加入淡奶，拌勻熱食。

● **心得：**

花生要焗透，才能煮出香味撲鼻之花生糊，但如太生或過火，糖水便會留'腥'味或苦味。

◆ **Ingredients:**

4 oz (100g) peanuts
5 cups water
5 oz (150g) rock sugar
2 tablespoons rice
2 oz (50ml) evaporated milk

◆ **Method:**

1. Roast peanuts in 150°C preheated oven for 15-20 minutes until cooked, cool and remove skin. Blend with 1 cup of water in an electric blender, filter to a fine peanut solution.
2. Soften rice in ½ of cup water, blend and drain to get a fine rice solution.
3. Bring the rest of water to boil, dissolve rock sugar, add peanut mixture, stir and simmer for 1 minute.
4. Thicken with rice solution, add evaporated milk, mix well, serve hot.

● **Practical Tip:**

Peanuts should be well-cooked and brown in the oven, a raw or burnt flavour will be left in the sweet tea if peanuts are under-cooked or over-roasted.

份量：8碗
製作時間：45分鐘
To make: 8 bowls
Work Time: 45 minutes

芝麻糊

◆ 材料：

黑芝麻5安士（150克），白米4湯匙，片糖8安士（225克），水6杯。

◆ 製法：

1. 芝麻預早一天洗淨，去沙，瀝乾水分，吹乾後用白鑊炒香。
2. 白米洗淨，用1杯水浸1小時，放入攪拌機內攪成米漿，過濾候用。
3. 黑芝麻用1½杯水攪至極幼，用密篩過濾成幼滑芝麻漿。
4. 將3½杯水燒滾，加入片糖，煮至糖溶，加入芝麻漿，慢火煮片刻，拌入適量米漿，煮至稠。
5. 離火熱食。

● 心得：

如隔渣用之篩不夠密，可將隔出之芝麻漿再過濾一次，務求達至幼滑之效果。

◆ **Ingredients:**

5 oz (150g) black sesame
4 tablespoons rice
8 oz (225g) slab sugar
6 cups water

◆ **Method:**

1. Rinse black sesame to clean, drain and air-dry overnight. Brown in a dry clean wok over a medium heat.
2. Soak rice in 1 cup water for 1 hour, blend and drain to form a fine rice solution.
3. Blend black sesame in 1 ½ cups water to form a fine solution, pass through a fine sieve.
4. Dissolve slab sugar in remaining water, add sesame solution, stir and cook for a while.
5. Serve hot.

● **Practical Tip:**

If drainer or sieve is not fine enough, drain the sesame solution twice to get a smooth and fine result.

CASHEW NUT SWEET TEA

份量：8碗
製作時間：30分鐘
To make: 8 bowls
Work Time: 30 minutes

◆ **材料：**

腰果8安士(225克)，鹽½茶匙、水3杯(焓腰果用)，白米1湯匙，水6杯，冰糖6安士(175克)。

◆ **製法：**

1. 腰果原粒放入鹽水內焓2分鐘，取出，隔清水份，吹乾後放暖油內炸至浮起及呈微金黃色(以微爆開為合)，撈起吸去多餘油分。
2. 白米用½杯水浸透，放入攪拌機攪成米漿，過濾。
3. 將炸好的腰果及1½杯水放入攪拌機攪成腰果漿。
4. 將餘下之4杯水煮滾，加入冰糖煮溶，加入腰果漿及適量米漿，煮至微稠即可供吃。

● **心得：**

炸腰果時不宜炸過火，否則糖水會帶燶味；用鹽水焓過腰果可去"青"味。煮腰果露時須不停攪拌，否則很易黏煲底。腰果含澱粉質較其他果仁高，不宜加太多米漿，也可隨意加入少量淡奶，但不宜太多，否則會太膩口。

◆ **Ingredients:**

8 oz (225g) cashew nuts
½ teaspoon salt and 3 cups water (for boiling cashew nut)
1 tablespoon rice
6 cups water
6 oz (175g) rock sugar

◆ **Method:**

1. Boil cashew nuts in salt solution for 2 minutes, drain and air-dry. Deep-fry until golden brown. Remove and drain.
2. Soak rice in ½ cup of water for 1 hour. Blend to form rice solution, drain well.
3. Blend fried cashew nuts in 1½ cups water to get a fine solution.
4. Dissolve rock sugar in the remaining water, add cashew nuts and thicken slightly with rice solution, mix well, serve hot.

● **Practical Tip:**

Boiling cashew nuts in salt water helps to remove the raw flavour. Do not over-cook cashew nuts to avoid a "burnt" taste in the sweet tea. Cashew nut contains a high percentage of starch, keep stirring to avoid sticking and do not over-thicken the dessert.

份量：10碗
製作時間：20分鐘
To make: 10 bowls
Work Time: 20 minutes

馬

◆ **材料：**

去衣馬蹄1磅(450克)，清水5杯，冰糖8安士(225克)，馬蹄粉2湯匙，蛋2隻(打勻)。

◆ **製法：**

1. 馬蹄磨成茸，或拍扁剁碎。
2. 冰糖加水煮溶，加入馬蹄茸煮滾，除去泡沫。
3. 馬蹄粉加水2湯匙開溶，加入糖水中煮至微稠。
4. 離火打入蛋汁，拌成蛋花，冷熱吃皆可。

● **心得：**

如想加入開邊綠豆，可預先將豆浸透，用大火蒸熟，約20分鐘，取出與馬蹄茸一同放入糖水中便可。

◆ **Ingredients:**

1 lb. (450g) peeled waterchestnut
5 cups water
8 oz (225g) rock sugar
2 tablespoons water chestnut flour
2 beaten eggs

◆ **Method:**

1. Grate or crush and chop waterchestnut.
2. Bring water and rock sugar to boil, add waterchestnut, remove foam when re-boils.
3. Mix waterchestnut flour with 2 tablespoons water. Add to syrup, stir till thickened.
4. Remove from heat, stir in beaten egg. Serve either hot or cold.

● **Practical Tip:**

Some people like to add green split beans in the syrup. Soak, drain and steam the split beans over high heat for about 20 minutes or until cooked, add into boiling syrup, stir well and serve.

OATMEAL PORRIDGE

份量：2人
製作時間：15分鐘
To serve: 2
Work Time: 15 minutes

麥皮奶糊

◆ **材料：**
快熟麥片6湯匙，煉奶4湯匙，水2½杯，蛋1隻。

◆ **製法：**
1. 快熟麥片用½杯冷水開溶，加入2杯滾水內，邊煮邊攪至微稠。
2. 拌入煉奶，離火打入蛋花即可。

● **心得：**
若喜歡的話，食譜可稍作變化。你大可加入各式水果，如雜果、蜜桃、切片香蕉等，便成另一款小吃。

◆ **Ingredients:**
6 tablespoons instant oatmeal
4 tablespoons condensed milk
2½ cups water
1 beaten egg

◆ **Method:**
1. Mix oatmeal with ½ cup of cold water, mix into 2 cups boiling water, stir well till thickens.
2. Add condensed milk, mix well, remove from heat, add beaten egg, mix and serve.

● **Practical Tip:**
If desired, variations can be done by adding mixed fruit, such as sliced apricots, peaches and bananas.

份量：12碗
製作時間：45分鐘
To make: 12 bowls
Work Time: 45 minutes

荔芋西米露

◆ 材料：

荔甫芋10安士（275克），西米4安士（100克），冰糖6安士（175克），水2½杯，淡奶½杯，椰汁¾杯。

◆ 製法：

1. 荔甫芋去皮後切粒，用大火蒸熟，趁熱壓成芋茸，或原粒使用。
2. 西米用大滾水浸15分鐘，間中攪拌使不黏作一團，瀝乾後置滾水內煮至半透明，瀝乾沖冷水候用。
3. 冰糖加水煮滾，加入已沖透之西米及芋茸，煮滾，離火伴入椰汁及淡奶，趁熱進食。

● 心得：

西米只需煮至半透明便可離火，一經沖冷水便完全呈透明狀。

◆ **Ingredients:**

10 oz (275g) taro
4 oz (100g) sago
6 oz (175g) rock sugar
2 ½ cups water
½ cup evaporated milk
¾ cup coconut milk

◆ **Method:**

1. Peel and dice taro, steam over high heat until cooked. Mash while still hot or just use the diced taro.
2. Soak sago in boiling water for 15 minutes, stir occassionally. Drain and boil until almost cooked, keep stirring. Drain, rinse under tap water and drain again.
3. Dissolve rock sugar in water, add sago and mashed taro, stir until re-boils. Remove from heat, stir in evaporated milk and coconut milk. Serve hot.

● **Practical Tip:**

Start rinsing sago under tap water when there is still a white spot in the centre. It will turn to transparent once in cold water. Drain and use.

STEWED WHITE FUNGI WITH ARILLUS LONGAN IN SYRUP

份量：8碗
製作時間：2小時15分鐘
To make: 8 bowls
Work Time: 2 hours 15 minutes

元肉銀耳露

◆ 材料：

雪耳1½安士(40克)，乾龍眼肉1½安士(40克)，南杏北杏2湯匙，冰糖6安士(175克)，薑汁2茶匙，滾水6杯。

◆ 製法：

1. 雪耳浸軟，剪去硬蒂，分成小朵，洗淨瀝乾，置大滾水內略拖，過冷水，瀝乾候用。
2. 龍眼肉洗淨，南杏北杏略浸。
3. 將所有材料置燉盅內，注入滾水，加蓋(可用鋁箔，即俗稱錫紙)隔水燉2小時即可，冷熱吃皆可。

● 心得：

雪耳可配木瓜同燉，或清燉冰糖，離火後加椰汁，配搭可隨個人口味而變化。

◆ **Ingredients:**

1½ oz (40g) white fungi
1½ oz (40g) dried arillus longan
2 tablespoons Chinese skinned almond
6 oz (175g) rock sugar (crushed)
2 teaspoons ginger juice
6 cups boiling water

◆ **Method:**

1. Soak white fungi till soft, remove stalks, divide into small flowerlets, wash and drain. Blanch in boiling water, rinse and drain again.
2. Rinse arillus longan and Chinese almond.
3. Put all ingredients in a casserole, add boiling water, cover and steam for 2 hours. Serve hot or cold.

● **Practical Tip:**

For variations, stew white fungi with diced papaya, or served plain white fungi syrup with coconut milk.

WALNUT PUDDING WITH CHINESE DATES

份量：10件
製作時間：30分鐘
To make: 10 pieces
Work Time: 30 minutes

南棗合桃糕

◆ **材料：**

南棗3安士（75克），連衣合桃肉5安士（150克），麥芽糖約¾杯（用熱水座軟），油1湯匙。

◆ **製法：**

1. 南棗洗淨，焓5－10分鐘，去衣去核吹乾，與合桃肉一同置深碗內，倒入適量麥芽糖，加油拌勻，迅速倒入方形膠盒內，壓平。
2. 待合桃糕結成硬塊後，取出切件即可。

● **心得：**

麥芽糖要座至軟身及呈流質狀才易與合桃料拌勻。

◆ **Ingredients:**

3 oz (75g) Chinese black dates
5 oz (150g) shelled walnuts
¾ cup, approximately malt syrup (soften over steaming water)
1 tablespoon oil

◆ **Method:**

1. Rinse and simmer black dates for 5-10 minutes. Remove skin and stone, air dry, mix with walnut, bind with sufficient amount of malt syrup, add oil, mix and pour into plastic box, flatten.
2. When harden and set, unmould walnut pudding, slice and serve.

● **Practical Tip:**

For easy mixing, malt syrup should be softened over high steam until a dripping consistency is obtained.

STEAMED MILK CUSTARD

份量：4碗
製作時間：30分鐘
To make: 4 bowls
Work Time: 30 minutes

鮮奶燉蛋

◆ **材料：**

蛋液1杯，水1杯，鮮奶1杯，冰糖4安士(100克)。

◆ **製法：**

1. 逐少拌入鮮奶於蛋液中。
2. 冰糖用水煮溶，待冷，加入蛋料中，過濾一次。
3. 將蛋料平均放入飯碗中，放入蒸籠慢火蒸至凝固(約25分鐘)，熱食。

● **心得：**

如用鑊蒸，可蓋上保鮮紙隔去水氣，需時約15－20分鐘便可。

◆ **Ingredients:**

1 cup beaten egg
1 cup water
1 cup fresh milk
4 oz (100g) rock sugar

◆ **Method:**

1. Add fresh milk into beaten egg gradually.
2. Dissolve rock sugar in 1 cup of water. Cool, gradually mix into the egg mixture and drain.
3. Divide mixture into 4 rice bowls, steam over gentle heat in a bamboo steamer for about 25 minutes or until set, serve hot.

● **Practical Tip:**

If a metal steamer or wok is used, cover custard with glad wrap to avoid water vapour. Cooking time is about 15-20 minutes.

份量：6件
製作時間：20分鐘
To make: 6 pieces
Work Time: 20 minutes

熱香餅

◆ 材料：

自發粉4安士(100克)，蛋2隻，鮮奶4安士(125毫升)，糖1湯匙。

◆ 伴食：

糖膠、牛油各少許。

◆ 製法：

1. 自發粉篩入大碗內，中間開穴，打入雞蛋及放入糖，逐少加入鮮奶，拌勻。
2. 隔去粉粒，置量杯內。
3. 平底鑊燒熱，加油少許，傾入適量麵漿，煎至兩面均呈金黃色。
4. 上碟，與牛油及糖膠同上。

● 心得：

熱香餅以糖膠及牛油伴吃乃傳統吃法。喜歡的話，可煎兩塊大小一樣的熱香餅，中間夾一層豆沙，便成為現今流行的"叮噹燒餅"了。

◆ **Ingredients:**

4 oz (100g) self-raising flour
2 eggs
4 oz (125ml) fresh milk
1 tablespoon castor sugar

◆ **To Serve:**

Some golden syrup and butter

◆ **Method:**

1. Sieve self-raising flour in a deep bowl, make a well in the centre, add sugar and drop in eggs. Gradually mix in fresh milk, stir well.
2. Drain to remove lumps, keep batter in a jug.
3. Heat a frying pan till hot, add a little oil, pour in sufficient batter, turn and fry until golden brown on both sides.
4. Dish and serve hot cakes with golden syrup and butter.

● **Practical Tip:**

For variations, sandwich two hot cakes with a layer of red bean paste as filling, and will become a popular Japanese "sweetie".

MANGO PUDDING

份量：6杯
製作時間：20分鐘
To make: 6 cups
Work Time: 20 minutes

芒果布甸

◆ **材料：**

芒果2個，魚膠粉1½湯匙，糖4安士（100克），熱水1½杯，鮮奶1杯，蛋黃2個。

◆ **製法：**

1. 芒果起肉切件，放入攪拌機內，加奶少許磨成芒果茸候用。
2. 魚膠粉與糖混合加入熱水內攪溶，或可座在一杯滾水上加速糖溶及避免魚膠粉起粒。
3. 蛋黃打勻，逐少加入鮮奶拌勻，混入魚膠糖水及芒果茸拌勻即可倒進啫喱杯內。
4. 將布甸凍至凝固，用鮮果或鮮忌廉同上。

● **心得：**

可將一個芒果切粒，另一個磨茸，以增口感。

◆ **Ingredients:**

2 mangoes
1 ½ tablespoon gelatine
4 oz (100g) sugar
1½ cup hot water
1 cup fresh milk
2 egg yolks

◆ **Method:**

1. Skin and remove stones of mangoes, blend with a little fresh milk to form mango pureé.
2. Mix gelatine and sugar in hot water, stir constantly over a pot of steaming water to form a clear gelatine syrup.
3. Beat egg yolks, gradually mix in fresh milk, add gelatine syrup and mango pureé, mix well, pour into jelly moulds.
4. Chill until set. Serve with selected fruit and fresh cream.

● **Practical Tip:**

Dice 1 of the mangoes and pureé the other one for variation.

份量：20個
製作時間：30分鐘
To make: 20 pieces
Work Time: 30 minutes

擂沙湯丸

◆ 材料：

糯米粉6安士（175克），粘米粉1安士（25克），豬油1湯匙，暖水¾杯，麻蓉8安士（225克），黃豆粉2杯。

◆ 製法：

1. 糯米粉與粘米粉拌勻，加入豬油及暖水，拌成一軟滑粉糰，搓長，分成20小份。
2. 麻蓉搓長亦分成20小粒。
3. 將粉糰搓圓按扁，加入麻蓉，埋口搓圓，置大滾水內煮至湯丸浮起。
4. 撈起瀝乾水分，趁熱滾上黃豆粉，熱食。

● 心得：

黃豆粉在點心用料專門店有售，但需大量購買。如不方便，可將珠豆焗香（焗爐溫度150°C），去衣後用電磨機磨成粉狀代替黃豆粉。

◆ **Ingredients:**

6 oz (175g) glutinous rice flour
1 oz (25g) rice flour
1 tablespoon lard
¾ cup warm water
8 oz (225g) sesame paste
2 cups soya bean powder

◆ **Method:**

1. Mix glutinous rice flour with rice flour, add lard and warm water to form a soft dough. Roll and divide into 20 equal portions.
2. Roll and divide sesame paste into 20 portions.
3. Roll and press the dough, stuff in sesame paste, seal and shape into a ball. Cook dumplings in fast boiling water.
4. Drain and coat with soya bean powder when still hot. Serve.

● **Practical Tip:**

Soya bean powder can only be obtained in bulb order from special suppliers. For convenience, ground roasted peanut can be used as alternate coating for the sweet dumplings.

COCONUT PUDDING

份量：20件
製作時間：1小時
To make: 20 pieces
Work Time: 1 hour

椰汁糕

1.將蛋白打至企身，逐少加入半凝固之魚膠奶糊
Whip egg white until stiff, gradually whip in gelatine mixture.

2.迅速倒入方盤，掃平，冷凍至凝固
Pour mixture in lined tin, make top smooth and chill until set.

◆ 材料：

水1杯(250毫升)，沙糖5安士(125克)，魚膠粉1安士(25克)，椰汁1杯(250毫升)，鮮奶1杯(250毫升)，蛋白6安士(150毫升)。

◆ 製法：

1. 燒滾水1杯，加入沙糖煮溶，離火待暖，輕拌入魚膠粉，攪至溶透，加入椰汁及鮮奶，置雪櫃內凍至半凝固如厚忌廉狀。
2. 蛋白置深碗內打至企身，逐少加入魚膠奶糊，打至材料完全混合。
3. 將混合物迅速倒入已墊了牛油紙的方盤內，凍至凝固後倒出，切件冷吃。

● 心得：

1. 如冷凍魚膠奶糊過久的話，可將它座在熱水上，便回復流質狀，再重新冷凍成忌廉狀即可。
2. 打蛋白時，不要太早加入魚膠奶糊，以免椰汁糕呈層次狀。可置冰塊上打匀，以加速混合。
3. 用電打蛋器製此甜品可省時及省力。

◆ Ingredients:

1 cup (250ml) water
5 oz (125g) castor sugar
1 oz (25g) gelatine
1 cup (250ml) coconut milk
1 cup (250ml) fresh milk
6 oz (150ml) egg white

◆ Method:

1. Boil water, add sugar, when dissolved, cool down a bit, add gelatine, stir well, add coconut milk and fresh milk, chill in the refrigerator until half set (like the consistency of thick cream).
2. Whip egg white in a deep bowl until stiff, gradually whip in gelatine mixture until ingredients are well mixed.
3. Immediately pour mixture in lined tin, chill until firm and set, cut into pieces, serve cold.

● Practical Tips:

1. If gelatine mixture is over-set, melt over steaming water and re-chill to get a creamy consistency.
2. Never pour gelatine mixture into egg white until egg white is stiff enough to hold the mixture. Add gradually and beat on top of ice cubes to speed up blending.
3. Whipping with an electric blender can save time and energy.

SPLIT PEA PUDDING

份量：20件
製作時間：15分鐘
To make: 20 pieces
Work Time: 15 minutes

馬豆糕

◆ **材料：**

馬豆2安士（50克），粟粉3安士（75克），椰汁1杯（250毫升），鮮奶6安士（200毫升），大菜½安士（15克），水4杯（1公升），沙糖5安士（125克）。

◆ **製法：**

1. 預備方形糕盤，用冷水搪過。
2. 馬豆用慢火焓稔，過冷水瀝乾候用。
3. 粟粉用椰汁及鮮奶開勻。
4. 大菜放4杯滾水內煮溶，過濾，離火加入沙糖及奶糊，開火攪至濃稠，滾後加馬豆。
5. 將奶糊倒入糕盤內，待冷雪凍，倒出切件冷吃。

● **心得：**

用紅豆代替馬豆，便成為另一款糕品了。煮紅豆之水可留作煮大菜用。

◆ **Ingredients:**

2 oz (50g) yellow split peas
3 oz (75g) cornstarch
1 cup (250ml) coconut milk
6 oz (200ml) fresh milk
½ oz (15g) agar agar
4 cups (1 litre) water
5 oz (125g) castor sugar

◆ **Method:**

1. Rinse square tins with cold water.
2. Simmer yellow split peas until soft. Rinse and drain.
3. Mix cornstarch with coconut milk and fresh milk.
4. Dissolve agar-agar in 4 cups boiling water, drain, stir in sugar and milk solution. When thickens, add yellow split peas.
5. Pour mixture in square tin, cool and chill. Unmould, slice and serve cold.

● **Practical Tip:**

For variations, use cooked red beans instead of yellow split peas.

份量：10件
製作時間：1小時
To make: 10 pieces
Work Time: 1 hour

◆ **Ingredients:**

3 oz (75g) red beans
2 tablespoons gelatine
6 tablespoons castor sugar
10 oz (300ml) boiling water

◆ **Method:**

1. Soak red bean for several hours, drain and put into a deep bowl. Add boiling water to cover the beans and steam over high heat for 1 hour until tender. Drain excessive water. Let cool.
2. Mix gelatine with sugar. Pour in 10 oz (300ml) boiling water. Stir until gelatine is well dissolved.
3. Pour a layer of gelatine solution in a plastic box to ½ cm thick. Set in the freezer for about 15-20 minutes.
4. Mix the remaining gelatine solution with the cooked red beans. Spread on top of set jelly. Chill for 4-5 hours.
5. Unmould, cut into pieces, serve cold.

● **Practical Tip:**

Stewing helps to keep beans in shape. Boiling saves cooking time but beans will become too soft.

◆ **材料：**

紅豆3安士（75克），魚膠粉2滿湯匙，沙糖6湯匙，滾水10安士（300毫升）。

◆ **製法：**

1. 紅豆浸透，置深碗內，注入浸過面之滾水，大火燉1小時至豆稔為止。隔去多餘水分，待冷。
2. 魚膠粉與沙糖拌勻，注入滾水10安士（300毫升）不停攪拌至魚膠粉溶透。
3. 預備方形膠盒，注入一層魚膠糖水，約½厘米厚，置雪櫃內凍15－20分鐘至凝固。
4. 將餘下之魚膠糖水加入已燉好之紅豆內拌勻，鋪在已凝固之啫喱上，置雪櫃內冷凍4－5小時。
5. 取出紅豆糕，切件冷吃。

● **心得：**

紅豆隔水燉稔可保持原粒狀；將紅豆煲熟較省時但易爆裂。

香炸小食

DEEP-FRIED SNACKS

SHRIMP TOAST

份量：12件
製作時間：45分鐘
To make: 12 pieces
Work Time: 45 minutes

◆ **材料：**

中蝦12安士(350克)，免治豬肉3安士(75克)，白方飽3片，蛋白2茶匙，白芝麻2湯匙。

◆ **調味料：**

鹽¼茶匙，粟粉2茶匙，胡椒粉少許。

◆ **製法：**

1. 蝦去殼去腸，用生粉略醃，再沖洗乾淨，吸乾水分，用刀拍成蝦膠，加入免治豬肉及調味料，拌至起膠，置雪櫃內凍片刻。
2. 方飽去皮，鈒成圓形多士或切成三角形共12塊，每塊釀上適量餡料掃平，沾上蛋白及白芝麻，壓實。
3. 將蝦多士放入中火油鑊，餡料向下，炸至熟透及呈金黃色，瀝乾油分熱食。

● **心得：**

炸蝦多士之油溫要適中，太熱麵飽易"燶"，太冷則令麵飽吸滿油，最好先用竹筷子試油溫，有小泡微開便可將多士逐件放入。

◆ **Ingredients:**

12 oz (350g) medium prawns
3 oz (75g) minced pork
3 slices white bread
2 teaspoons egg white
2 tablespoons white sesame

◆ **Seasonings:**

¼ teaspoon salt
2 teaspoons cornstarch
Dash of pepper

◆ **Method:**

1. Shell and devein prawns, marinate with a little cornstarch, rinse and pat dry. Crush with a chopper to form shrimp paste, mix in minced pork and seasonings. Stir until sticky, chill for 10-15 minutes.
2. Remove crust from white bread, cut in twelve triangular or round toasts, spread a teaspoonful of filling on one side. Dampen slightly with egg white and dust with white sesame. Press well.
3. Deep-fry toast in medium oil with filling face downward till cooked and golden brown. Drain and serve hot.

● **Practical Tip:**

Test the temperature of oil with a bamboo chopstick, when there are tiny bubbles running up, oil is ready. Bread will become too soggy in cold oil but brown immediately when oil is overheated.

份量：20條
製作時間：45分鐘
To make: 20 pieces
Work Time: 45 minutes

春卷

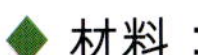

◆ **材料：**

急凍春卷皮10塊；蒜頭1粒；冬菇4隻；甘筍絲2安士（50克）；瘦肉絲4安士（100克）；韮黃1安士（25克）。

◆ **黏口用：**

麵粉2茶匙與水1湯匙拌勻。

◆ **調味料：**

鹽½茶匙，糖½茶匙，生抽1茶匙，蠔油1湯匙，生粉1滿茶匙，水4湯匙。

◆ **蘸料：**

喼汁少許。

◆ **製法：**

1. 瘦肉絲加油、生粉及水各少許略醃；蒜頭略拍；冬菇浸軟後切絲；甘筍絲出水；韮黃切段。
2. 用1湯匙油起鑊，爆香蒜頭棄掉，加入冬菇絲、肉絲及甘筍絲略炒1分鐘，加入調味料，炒透，離火加入韮黃段，盛起待冷。
3. 春卷皮平放，其中一角向枱邊，放入適量餡料，先將左右兩邊覆上，再自前方向上捲起，用麵粉糊埋口。
4. 春卷放入中火油濫，炸時需經常轉動。
5. 取出瀝乾油分，可中間斜切開，用喼汁伴吃。

● **心得：**

餡料要冷透才可包入春卷皮，否則春卷易穿口。

◆ **Ingredients:**

10 sheets frozen spring roll wrappers
1 clove garlic
4 Chinese mushrooms
2 oz (50g) shredded carrot
4 oz (100g) shredded pork
1 oz (25g) yellow chives

◆ **For sealing:**

2 teaspoons plain flour mix with 1 tablespoon water

◆ **Seasonings:**

½ teaspoon salt
½ teaspoon sugar
1 teaspoon light soya sauce
1 tablespoon oyster sauce
1 level teaspoon cornstarch
4 tablespoons water

◆ **Dipping:**

Worcestershire sauce to taste

◆ **Method:**

1. Mix shredded pork with a little oil, cornstarch and water. Crush garlic; soak Chinese mushrooms until soft, shred. Blanch the shredded carrot. Cut yellow chives into 2cm lengths.
2. Heat 1 tablespoon oil in wok, sauté crushed garlic, discard. Add shredded mushroom, pork and carrot, stir for 1 minute, add seasonings, fry until thickened, add yellow chives, mix, dish and cool.
3. Place sufficient filling on the centre of each spring roll wrapper, lift and bring both sides of wrappers over each other, roll from bottom up to the top to form a cylinder, seal with a little plain flour mixture.
4. Deep-fry spring rolls over moderate heat, move spring rolls constantly.
5. Dish, drain, cut into halves, serve with worcestershire sauce.

● **Practical Tip:**

Filling should be cooled thoroughly for easy wrapping.

CURRY BEEF TRIANGLES

份量：12件
製作時間：45分鐘
To make: 12 pieces
Work Time: 45 minutes

咖喱角

◆ Ingredients:

12 sheets frozen spring roll wrappers
4 oz (100g) minced beef
½ onion
1 level tablespoon curry paste

◆ For sealing:

1 tablespoon plain flour mix with 1 tablespoon water

◆ Seasonings:

¼ teaspoon salt
½ teaspoon sugar
1 teaspoon light soya sauce
Dash of sesame oil

◆ Cornstarch solution:

2 teaspoons cornstarch mix with 1 tablespoon water

◆ Method:

1. Trim spring roll wrappers to long strips of 4-5 cm wide, cover and set aside. Season minced beef. Dice the onion.
2. Heat 1 tablespoon oil in wok, sauté curry paste, add diced onion and seasoned minced beef, stir to cook well. Thicken with cornstarch solution. Dish, cool and chill.
3. Fold each end of stripped wrappers twice to form a triangle pocket, add 1 teaspoonful of filling, turn and fold to form triangle puff. Deep-fry till crispy. Serve hot.

● Practical Tip:

Spring roll wrappers should be well defrosted for easy separating.

◆ 材料：

急凍春卷皮12塊；免治牛肉4安士(100克)；洋葱半個；咖喱醬1滿湯匙。

◆ 黏口用：

麵粉1湯匙與水1湯匙拌勻。

◆ 調味料：

鹽¼茶匙，糖½茶匙，生抽1茶匙，麻油少許。

◆ 生粉水：

生粉2茶匙，水1湯匙。

◆ 製法：

1. 將春卷皮剪成4－5厘米闊之長條，蓋好候用；牛肉調味；洋葱切碎。
2. 用1湯匙油起鑊，爆香咖喱醬，加入洋葱碎及牛肉，炒片刻埋生粉水，盛起待冷雪凍。
3. 將春卷皮之一端摺兩下，成一三角袋形，放入牛肉餡，向前覆掃，最末端用麵粉糊埋口即可放入中火油內炸脆。

● 心得：

未完全解凍的春卷皮很易被撕爛，要待春卷皮軟化後才可逐塊分開。

CRISPY STUFFED BEAN CURD PUFF

份量：30件
製作時間：30分鐘
To make: 30 pieces
Work Time: 30 minutes

炸金花

◆ 材料：

鯪魚肉12安士(350克)，蝦膠4安士(100克)，豆腐卜15個，喼汁(伴食用)。

◆ 調味料：

鹽¾茶匙，糖¼茶匙，粟粉2茶匙，麻油少許，胡椒粉少許。

◆ 製法：

1. 鯪魚肉與蝦膠拌勻，加調味料，攪至起膠。
2. 將豆腐卜一開二，反轉裏面向外成袋形，釀入適量餡料，放熱油中炸至香脆，撈起，用喼汁伴食。

● 心得：

將豆腐卜反轉令豆腐向外炸起會更鬆脆，其狀似花球，故以"金花"命名。蘸料也可以茄汁或沙律醬代替。

◆ Ingredients:

12 oz (350g) minced fish
4 oz (100g) shelled prawns (mashed)
15 bean curd puffs
A little worchestershire sauce (to dip)

◆ Seasonings:

¾ teaspoon salt
¼ teaspoon sugar
2 teaspoons cornstarch
Dash of sesame oil
Shakes of pepper

◆ Method:

1. Mix minced fish and mashed prawns together, season, stir to a sticky paste.
2. Cut bean curd puffs into halves, turn inside out to form a pocket, stuff with filling, shape and deep-fry in hot oil until cooked and crispy. Drain and serve with worchestershire sauce.

● Practical Tip:

Worchestershire sauce can be substituted by tomato ketchup or salad dressing.

份量：24個
製作時間：20分鐘
To make: 24 pieces
Work Time: 20 minutes

炸蛋球

這裏介紹的炸蛋球體積小巧，容易入口，用來招呼客人或弄給小孩子吃，都方便得多，比對起在食肆中吃的「沙翁」，個子大大的一碟只能放一到兩個，小孩子吃起來弄得滿嘴滿臉都是糖粉，要勞動侍應取濕毛巾來抹手抹臉，顯然是「有文化」得多了。

1.水滾，加豬油，迅速傾入麵粉，離火攪成厚麵糊
Bring water and lard to boil, remove from heat, quickly stir in sifted flour to form a thick paste.

2.將蛋逐隻倒入，大力攪拌成一厚團
Add egg one by one, stir vigorously to form a thick mixture.

3.逐匙放入蛋球，慢火炸至蛋球脹大及微爆口，炸透後撈起趁熱捲上砂糖
Spoon mixture in warm oil, keep deep-frying until egg puffs burst and expand to 3 times larger. Drain and coat egg puffs with castor sugar when still hot.

◆ 材料：

清水6安士(200毫升)，豬油1¼安士(40克)，麵粉3½安士(80克)，蛋3隻，砂糖1杯。

◆ 製法：

1. 燒滾清水，加入豬油待溶，離火，迅速篩入麵粉，不停攪動，以不起粉粒為合。
2. 立刻將蛋逐隻拌入，攪成稠糊狀。
3. 燒油至暖，將麵糊逐匙加入，慢火炸至蛋球脹大3倍及微爆口，瀝乾油分。
4. 趁熱蘸上砂糖即可。

● 心得：

煮蛋糊時份量要準確，動作要迅速，蛋汁必須分次放入才較易將材料混合，記得離火。蛋球脹大只靠拌入之空氣，所以攪拌之動作很重要。油溫若過猛，會過早將蛋球之外皮硬化，空氣衝不出來，不能達至爆口效果，中心太軟難熟，所以火候也是炸蛋球關鍵之處。

◆ Ingredients:

6 oz (200ml) water
1¾ oz (40g) lard
3½ oz (80g) plain flour
3 eggs
1 cup castor sugar

◆ Method:

1. Bring water and lard to boil, remove from heat, sieve the flour, stir in sieved flour quickly, stir vigorously to avoid lumps.
2. Stir in eggs separately to form a thick paste.
3. Heat oil to lukewarm, scoop in flour mixture teaspoonful by teaspoonful. Deep-fry over gentle heat until egg puffs burst and expand to 3 times of the original size. Drain well.
4. Coat with castor sugar when still hot. Serve.

● Practical Tip:

Ingredients should be weighed accurately. Remember to add flour away from heat, eggs should be stirred in separately and vigorously. The expanding of egg puff depends on the amount of air trapped in the mixture, so steps should be followed continuously. The hard crust is caused by over-heated oil that prevents air to burst and a sticky uncooked puff will be resulted. Heat control of oil is another critical caution.

FRIED MILK CUSTARD

份量：15件
製作時間：1小時
To make: 15 pieces
Work Time: 1 hour

炸鮮奶

◆ 材料：
粟粉1½安士(40克)，鮮奶12安士(375毫升)，蛋白2隻，油1湯匙，鹽少許，糖½茶匙。

◆ 脆漿：
麵粉3安士(75克)，粟粉1½安士(40克)，發粉1茶匙，鹽少許，油1湯匙，水½杯。

◆ 伴食：
砂糖½杯。

◆ 製法：
1. 將粟粉及鮮奶拌勻加油及鹽和糖作調味，慢火煮成糊狀，須不停攪拌，待滾。
2. 離火，分3次快手攪入蛋白，拌勻，倒入已塗油的方形糕盤內，待冷，置雪櫃凍1－2小時。
3. 將脆漿料拌勻，靜置片刻。
4. 倒出鮮奶糕，切件，沾上脆漿置八成熱油內炸至香脆及呈金黃色。瀝乾油分，沾上砂糖熱食。

● 心得：
此脆漿可作多種用途，如炸豬扒、雞翼等。

◆ **Ingredients:**
1½ oz (40g) cornstarch
12 oz (375ml) fresh milk
2 egg whites (beaten)
1 tablespoon oil
Pinch of salt
½ teaspoon sugar

◆ **Batter:**
3 oz (75g) plain flour
1½ oz (40g) cornstarch
1 teaspoon baking powder
Pinch of salt
1 tablespoon oil
½ cup water

◆ **To serve:**
½ cup castor sugar

◆ **Method:**
1. Mix cornstarch with fresh milk, add oil, season with salt and sugar. Stir constantly over gentle heat until cooked.
2. Remove from heat, add beaten egg white gradually, stir between each addition. Mix well to form a smooth mixture, pour into a greased square tin. Cool and set in the refrigerator for 1-2 hours.
3. Mix batter ingredients to a thick consistency. Set aside.
4. Unmould milk custard, cut into cubes, coat with batter. Deep-fry over medium-high heat till set, crispy and golden brown. Drain, dip with castor sugar. Serve hot.

● **Practical Tip:**
This coating batter can be used for fried pork chop and chicken wings.

份量：10個
製作時間：1小時30分鐘
To make: 10 buns
Work Time: 1 hour 30 minutes

◆ 材料：

麵粉8安士(225克)，沙糖1湯匙，豬油1湯匙，乾依士½茶匙，發粉½茶匙，暖水½杯。

◆ 蘸料：

煉奶少許。

◆ 製法：

1. 乾依士及發粉加入暖水內和勻候用。
2. 麵粉與沙糖同篩入大碗內，中間開穴，倒入依士水及豬油，拌勻搓至軟滑，蓋好靜置1小時。
3. 將麵糰搓成長條，用刀切成小饅頭，再蓋好待10分鐘，使其質地鬆軟，置蒸籠內大火蒸15分鐘。
4. 取出饅頭待冷卻後置中火油內炸至呈金黃色即可，與煉奶同上。

● 心得：

麵糰待發的時間不定，須視乎室溫而定，如見輕微發起及軟身即可。如見麵糰有小氣泡狀即已發過久，蒸出來之饅頭便不夠理想。

◆ Ingredients:

8 oz (225g) plain flour
1 tablespoon castor sugar
1 tablespoon lard
½ teaspoon dry yeast
½ teaspoon baking powder
½ cup warm water

◆ To dip:

A little condensed milk

◆ Method:

1. Mix dry yeast and baking powder in warm water.
2. Sieve plain flour and castor sugar in a deep bowl, make a well in the centre, add yeast solution and lard, mix and knead to form a soft dough. Cover and proof for 1 hour.
3. Knead and roll dough to a long sausage form, cut into mini buns. Keep buns in a bamboo steamer, cover for 10 minutes for softening the texture. Steam over strong heat for 15 minutes.
4. Cool and deep-fry buns until crispy and golden brown. Serve with condensed milk.

● Practical Tip:

When tiny air bubbles are found in dough, it is over risen. Dough is ready when it becomes springy and soft. Time for proving depends upon room temperature.

TURNIP CAKES

份量：18個
製作時間：30分鐘
To make: 18 pieces
Work Time: 30 minutes

蘿蔔絲餅

◆ **材料：**

白蘿蔔10安士(275克)；蝦米2湯匙；葱粒2棵量；麵粉4安士(100克)，粘米粉1½安士(40克)，發粉½茶匙；清水1杯。

◆ **調味料：**

鹽¾茶匙，五香粉½茶匙，胡椒粉少許，麻油1茶匙。

◆ **製法：**

1. 麵粉、粘米粉及發粉篩好。
2. 蘿蔔刨絲，蝦米浸軟，切碎，放入調味料及葱粒拌勻，置筲箕內醃片刻，以去掉多餘水分。
3. 粉料與清水開勻成粉漿，加油、鹽及胡椒粉各少許，拌勻。
4. 燒油一鑊，放進長柄模型燒熱。
5. 將蘿蔔料加入粉漿內拌勻，當油燒至八成熱時，取出熱餅模，滴乾油分，加入適量蘿蔔漿，放回油中炸至離模及呈餅狀。
6. 將蘿蔔餅炸至鬆脆及呈金黃色，吸乾油分熱食。

● **心得：**

每次加入粉漿時必須將模燒熱，蘿蔔餅才易鬆脫。

◆ **Ingredients:**

10 oz (275g) turnip
2 tablespoons dried shrimps
2 stalks spring onion
4 oz (100g) plain flour
1½ oz (40g) rice flour
½ teaspoon baking powder
1 cup water

◆ **Seasonings:**

¾ teaspoon salt
½ teaspoon five-spice powder
Dash of pepper
1 teaspoon sesame oil

◆ **Method:**

1. Sieve plain flour, rice flour and baking powder together.
2. Grate the turnips; soak and dice the dried shrimps. Mix them with seasonings and diced spring onion, leave in colander to drip dry mixture.
3. Mix powdery ingredients with water to form a smooth batter, sprinkle in a little pepper, salt and oil, stir well.
4. Heat oil, slide in a metal mould until the mould is heated through.
5. Add the turnip mixture into the batter, lift and drain the heated mould, half-fill the mould with mixture, leave in medium-hot oil, unmould when an outer coat is formed.
6. Deep-fry turnip cakes until crispy and golden brown. Drain and serve.

● **Practical Tip:**

The mould should be heated through in between each addition of batter mixture to prevent sticking.

份量：8件
製作時間：20分鐘
To make: 8 pieces
Work Time: 20 minutes

腐皮蝦卷

◆ **材料：**

腐皮1塊，蝦膠8安士(225克)，蛋白1隻。

◆ **調味料：**

胡椒粉少許，鹽¼茶匙，生粉2茶匙。

◆ **製法：**

1. 腐皮用濕布抹淨，剪去硬邊，修成8塊正方形之腐皮，用布蓋好候用。
2. 蝦膠調味，打至起膠後置雪櫃內凍數小時。
3. 蝦膠分成8份；腐皮逐塊以菱形放平，放一份蝦膠於中央，先將兩邊摺入，再自前方捲起，以少許蛋白埋口。
4. 用中火油將腐皮卷炸脆即成，趁熱享用。

● **心得：**

若要蝦膠爽口彈牙，必須選購新鮮的中蝦，去殼去腸後要用生粉略擦再沖去潺滑之黏物及吸乾水。

拍成膠後最好放雪櫃內凍半日或過夜。

◆ **Ingredients:**

1 bean curd sheet
8 oz (225g) shrimp paste
1 beaten egg white

◆ **Seasonings:**

Shakes of pepper
¼ teaspoon salt
2 teaspoons cornstarch

◆ **Method:**

1. Wipe bean curd sheet clean, remove hard rims, trim into 8 squares. Cover with damp cloth.
2. Season shrimp paste, stir well. Chill for several hours.
3. Divide shrimp paste into 8 portions, line bean curd sheet flat, put a portion of shrimp paste in the centre. Fold from the sides and roll forward, seal with egg white.
4. Deep-fry bean curd rolls over medium heat until crispy. Serve hot.

● **Practical Tip:**

To prepare a crunchy shrimp paste, use medium fresh prawns. Rub shelled and deveined prawns with cornstarch, rinse and dry through before crushing. Chill shrimp paste for ½ to 1 day before use.

JUMBO WONTONS WITH SWEET AND SOUR SAUCE

份量：20件
製作時間：1小時
To make: 20 pieces
Work Time: 1 hour

錦鹵雲吞

◆ **材料：**
錦鹵雲吞皮20塊，蝦肉8安士（225克）。

◆ **調味料：**
鹽⅛茶匙，生粉1茶匙，胡椒粉少許，蛋黃½隻。

◆ **錦鹵料：**
蝦肉4安士（100克），叉燒2安士（50克），鮮魷魚1隻，雞肝1個，洋葱½個，青椒½個，尖紅椒1隻，菠蘿2片。

◆ **甜酸芡：**
水1杯，白醋1杯，茄汁½杯，喼汁1茶匙，糖½杯，鹽½茶匙。

◆ **生粉水：**
生粉1½湯匙，水2湯匙。

◆ **製法：**
1. 將8安士蝦肉吸乾水分後切粒，加入調味料拌勻並冷凍片刻，每塊雲吞皮包入少量餡料，對摺成多角形，於餡邊沿沾水少許埋口，置熱油內炸至鬆起及脹大，炸脆盛起。
2. 預備錦鹵料：將蝦肉出水；叉燒切片；魷魚洗淨，切花後切件，出水；雞肝出水後切件；洋葱、青椒、尖紅椒及菠蘿切塊；甜酸芡拌勻待用。
3. 燒油2湯匙，先爆香洋葱件，紅椒及青椒，炒片刻，加入其他材料，炒勻，倒入甜酸芡，煮滾埋生粉水煮稠，上碟。
4. 將炸好之雲吞蘸上甜酸芡，趁熱供吃。

● **心得：**
1. 錦鹵雲吞皮為特製之較大塊雲吞皮，內加適量臭粉，只宜油炸用，食其鬆脆之風味及蘸以特製之錦鹵芡，美味無窮。
2. 一般製麵店只供酒樓食館訂製錦鹵雲吞皮，家庭少量製作，可到粉麵店預先訂購，一般1－2天可有交易。

◆ **Ingredients:**
20 sheets wonton wrappers
8 oz (225g) shelled prawns

◆ **Seasonings:**
⅛ teaspoon salt
1 teaspoon cornstarch
Dash of pepper
½ egg yolk

◆ **Ingredients for Sweet and Sour Sauce:**
4 oz (100g) shelled shrimps
2 oz (50g) roast pork
1 squid
1 chicken liver
½ onion
½ green pepper
1 chilli
2 slices pineapple

◆ **Sweet and Sour Sauce:**
1 cup water
1 cup white vinegar
½ cup tomato ketchup
1 teaspoon worchestershire sauce
½ cup sugar
½ teaspoon salt

◆ **Thickening:**
1½ tablespoon cornstarch
2 tablespoons water

◆ **Method:**
1. Dry and dice 8 oz shelled prawns, add seasonings, mix and chill. Wrap a little filling in each wonton wrapper, fold diagonally and seal edge with water. Deep-fry wontons in hot oil until golden brown and crispy. Remove and drain.
2. Blanch shelled shrimps; slice the roast pork; score and cut the squid into pieces and blanch. Cut the chicken liver into pieces and blanch. Cut onion, green onion, chilli and pineapple slices into pieces. Mix sweet and sour sauce well.
3. Heat 2 tablespoons oil in wok, sauté onion, green pepper and chilli, stir well, add other ingredients and sweet and sour sauce, when boils, thicken with cornstarch solution.
4. Dish and serve hot with fried Jumbo Wontons.

● **Practical Tips:**
1. Wonton wrappers for deep-fry are specially made for a short and crispy result because of the amonnnia powder added in the flour dough. The Jumbo Wontons are specially served with sweet and sour sauce.
2. Wrappers for Jumbo Wontons should be ordered 1-2 days in advance from special noodles manufacturers.

份量：16件
製作時間：20分鐘
To make: 16 pieces
Work Time: 20 minutes

椒鹽豆腐

◆ **材料：**

實豆腐4件，淮鹽1茶匙。

◆ **脆漿料：**

自發粉4安士(100克)，冰水7安士(225毫升)，蔥粒1湯匙，紅椒碎1湯匙，鹽½茶匙。

◆ **蘸料：**

淮鹽少許。

◆ **製法：**

1. 實豆腐一開四，共十六件，灑上淮鹽略醃。
2. 將脆漿料拌勻，靜置片刻。
3. 豆腐吸乾水分，黏上脆漿料，置熱油內炸至鬆脆，蘸上淮鹽即食。

● **心得：**

此小食宜即炸即食，因豆腐的水分及熱氣會將脆皮軟化。但如果用大火將麵漿炸透至挺硬，就是多製幾件也無妨。

◆ **Ingredients:**

4 pieces firm bean curd
1 teaspoon spicy salt

◆ **Batter:**

4 oz (100g) self-raising flour
7 oz (225ml) iced water
1 tablespoon diced spring onion
1 tablespoon chopped chilli
½ teaspoon salt

◆ **To dip:**

A little spicy salt

◆ **Method:**

1. Quarter firm bean curds, season well with spicy salt.
2. Mix ingredients for batter, set aside for a while.
3. Drain bean curd, coat with batter, deep-fry in hot oil until golden brown. Drain and serve with spicy salt.

● **Practical Tip:**

The crispy coating tends to become limp in a short time because of the bean curd's softness and hot steam enclosed. Deep-fry the bean curd over a high heat until a hard crust is formed.

SPICY TARO

份量：15件
製作時間：20分鐘
To make: 15 pieces
Work Time: 20 minutes

酥炸芋片

◆ **材料：**

芋頭10安士(275克)。

◆ **麵糊：**

南乳汁1湯匙，五香粉½茶匙，自發粉4安士(100克)，鹽¼茶匙，蛋1隻，水3安士(75毫升)，油1茶匙。

◆ **製法：**

1. 芋頭去皮，洗淨後切成½厘米厚塊。
2. 將麵糊用料拌勻成炸漿，靜置片刻。
3. 燒油至熱，將芋片沾上炸漿，逐塊放入熱油中炸脆，瀝乾油分，熱食。

● **心得：**

將芋頭改為番薯塊，刪除麵糊內的南乳汁及五香粉，又變成另一款懷舊街頭小吃了。

◆ **Ingredients:**

10 oz (275g) taro

◆ **Batter:**

1 tablespoon red fermented bean curd sauce
½ teaspoon five-spice powder
4 oz (100g) self-raising flour
¼ teaspoon salt
1 egg
3 oz (75ml) water
1 teaspoon oil

◆ **Method:**

1. Peel, wash and cut taro into ½ cm thick slices.
2. Mix ingredients for batter together to form a thick coating consistency, rest for a while before use.
3. Heat oil, coat taro pieces with batter, deep-fry until cooked and golden brown, drain and serve.

● **Practical Tip:**

Substitute taro by sweet potato and omit five-spice powder and red fermented bean curd sauce in the batter for another traditional snack.

GOLDEN FISH BALLS

份量：8 個
製作時間：20 分鐘
To make: 8 pieces
Work Time: 20 minutes

炸鯪魚球

◆ **材料：**

鯪魚肉10安士（275克），果皮1小塊，鹽½茶匙，粟粉1湯匙，生抽½茶匙，糖½茶匙，胡椒粉少許，蛋白½隻，水2茶匙。

◆ **蘸料：**

蜆蚧醬。

◆ **製法：**

1. 果皮浸軟，去瓤後切碎。
2. 將所有材料拌勻，打至起膠，置雪櫃內凍2－4小時。
3. 魚膠分成8份，搓成丸狀，輕滾上生粉一層，置熱油內炸至魚熟及呈金黃色。
4. 撈起魚球，與蜆蚧醬同上，熱食。

● **心得：**

蜆蚧醬可到舊式之雜貨店，醬料專門店及中國國貨公司購買。

◆ **Ingredients:**

10 oz (275g) minced fish
1 small piece dried tangerine peel
½ teaspoon salt
1 tablespoon cornstarch
½ teaspoon light soya sauce
½ teaspoon sugar
Shakes of pepper
½ beaten egg white
2 teaspoons water

◆ **To Serve:**

Preserved clam meat paste

◆ **Method:**

1. Soak the dried tangerine peel till soft. Remove the pith and chop finely.
2. Mix all ingredients together. Stir until firm and sticky. Chill in the refrigerator for 2-4 hours.
3. Divide fish paste into 8 portions. Shape into round balls, slightly coat with cornstarch, deep-fry in hot oil until cooked and golden brown.
4. Dish and serve fish balls with preserved clam meat paste.

● **Practical Tip:**

Preserved clam meat paste is available in Chinese Emporiums and some of the traditional grocers.

酥炸合桃

合桃也就是「核桃」，不過香港人總喜歡用合桃這個俗稱而已。由於核桃營養豐富，故有「健康之友」的美譽，中醫說它有補血益精、潤肺補腎、斂肺定喘、止咳化痰、滋潤皮膚之功，可用於腎虧腰痛、健忘倦怠、食慾不振等症。既然如此，何不自己動手，在家中用核桃來製作一些健康而又美味的小食，讓家中的大小朋友都大快朵頤呢！

1.合桃用鹽水焓2分鐘後，放入糖水內煮1分鐘
Boil walnuts in salt solution for 2 minutes; drain, rinse and put into sugar solution.

2.將合桃炸脆
Deep-fry walnuts over medium-low heat.

◆ 材料：
無衣合桃肉10安士(275克)，沙糖5安士(125克)，水2安士(50毫升)。

◆ 糖漿：
糖膠1湯匙，蜜糖1湯匙，滾水2湯匙。

◆ 製法：
1. 合桃加滾水內，加鹽少許焓2分鐘，瀝乾沖淨，放入糖水內煮1分鐘，瀝去糖水，風乾。將糖漿材料拌勻。
2. 用慢火將合桃炸脆及呈金黃色撈起，趁熱淋上糖漿料，拌勻即可。

心得：
用鹽水焓合桃可令合桃更鬆脆。

◆ Ingredients:
10 oz (275g) skinned walnut
5 oz (125g) castor sugar
2 oz (50ml) water

◆ Syrup:
1 tablespoon golden syrup
1 tablespoon honey
2 tablespoons boiling water

◆ Method:
1. Bring walnut to boil with a pinch of salt for 2 minutes, drain and rinse. Put into sugar solution and boil for another minute, drain and air dry. Mix the syrup well.
2. Deep-fry walnuts over medium-low heat until crispy and golden brown, drain and immediately mix with syrup. Serve when cooled.

Practical Tip:
Boiling walnut in salt solution helps to enhance its crispiness.

份量：8-10塊
製作時間：30分鐘
To make: 8-10 patties
Work Time: 30 minutes

豆沙窩餅

豆沙窩餅在許多地方都可以吃得到，但不是皮太厚就是內裏的豆沙太少，如果自己動手做，就較有機會吃得滿意。

用作餡料的豆沙源於紅豆，那是一種一年生的草本植物的果實，有些人讀了王維的詩句：「紅豆生南國，春來發幾枝，勸君多採擷，此物最相思」，於是便自作聰明的在情信中夾附幾粒紅豆以比喻相思之意。但其實古詩中的紅豆是一種高大喬木的種子，與食用的紅豆截然不同，可千萬不要誤把馮京作馬涼呢！

1.將豆沙鋪在薄餅皮中央
Place red bean paste on centre of pancake sheet.

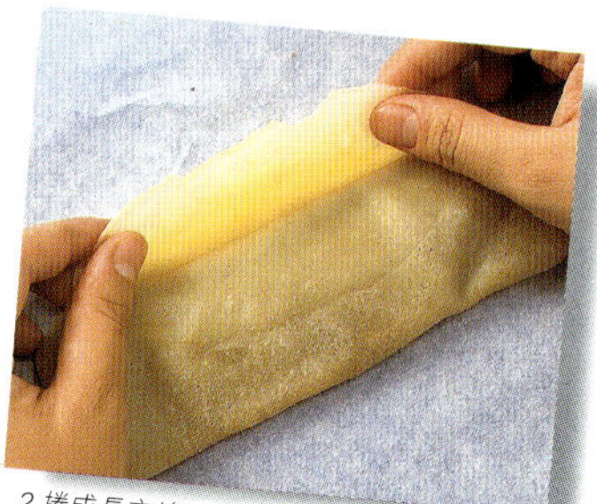

2.捲成長方塊，用少許麵糊黏口
Fold and press to form a flat patty, seal with a little batter.

◆ 材料：

麵粉5安士(150克)，蛋2隻，鮮奶1½杯，豆沙8安士(225克)。

◆ 製法：

1. 麵粉過篩，加蛋及鮮奶，開成稀滑奶漿，用平底鑊煎成8－10塊薄餅，只需煎一面，留少許粉漿作黏口用。
2. 將薄餅舖平，底向下，豆沙分成8－10份，逐份放上薄餅中央成長條形。
3. 自下方及兩邊餘位覆起，向前包成長扁狀，用少許粉漿黏口。
4. 燒熱油，用中火將豆沙窩餅炸至金黃色，撈起瀝乾油分，斬件趁熱享用。

● 心得：

此薄餅可作西式的"班戟"，佐以鮮果忌廉、吞拿魚或果醬用。

◆ Ingredients:

5 oz (150g) plain flour
2 eggs
1½ cups fresh milk
8 oz (225g) red bean paste

◆ Method:

1. Sieve flour, add eggs and fresh milk gradually, mix to form a smooth batter, fry into 8-10 pancakes sheets. Fry on one side only (reserve a little batter for sealing pancakes).
2. Lie pancake sheet flat, underside downward, divide red bean paste into 8-10 portions. Spread each portion on centre of pancake sheet.
3. Fold pancake from lower flap and sides, roll to a flat oblong, damp edge with reserved batter, press to seal edges.
4. Heat the wok, deep-fry red bean patties in medium-hot oil until golden brown. Dish, drain, cut into sections. Serve hot.

● Practical Tip:

The pancake sheet can also be served with fruit and fresh cream, tuna fish or jam.

精美鹹點

SAVOURY SNACKS

POTATO CAKES

份量：12個
製作時間：45分鐘
To make: 12 pieces
Work Time: 45 minutes

薯仔餅

◆ **材料：**

薯仔1磅(450克)，冬菇4隻，蝦米2湯匙，臘腸½條，葱粒1湯匙，蛋1隻，粟粉3湯匙。

◆ **調味料：**

鹽½茶匙，粟粉1湯匙，胡椒粉、麻油各少許。

◆ **製法：**

1. 薯仔洗淨，連皮浸沒過面之滾水內焓約20分鐘至熟，取出去皮，趁熱壓成薯茸。
2. 冬菇及蝦米浸軟，切細粒；臘腸蒸熟切幼粒與葱粒一同放入薯茸中，調味後分成12等份。
3. 將每份薯茸料搓圓按扁，掃上蛋液，輕拍上粟粉，置中火油鑊煎至薯餅兩面呈金黃色即可供吃。

● **心得：**

如想薯仔餅更顯香味，可將一半薯仔壓茸，一半切成粗粒互相混合，更可一新口感。

◆ **Ingredients:**

1 lb. (450g) potato
4 pieces dried mushroom
2 tablespoons dried shrimps
½ Chinese sausage
1 tablespoon diced spring onion
1 egg
3 tablespoons cornstarch

◆ **Seasonings:**

½ teaspoon salt
1 tablespoon cornstarch
A little pepper
A little sesame oil

◆ **Method:**

1. Scrub potato, put in a large pot of boiling water, boil approximately for 20 minutes till cooked, skin and mash to form potato cream.
2. Soak and dice dried mushroom and dried shrimps; steam Chinese sausage until cooked, dice finely and add into potato cream with diced spring onion, season, mix and divide into 12 equal portions.
3. Shape each portion of potato mixture into a round, press slightly, coat with beaten egg and cornstarch, shallow-fry over medium heat until cakes are golden brown on both sides. Serve.

● **Practical Tip:**

Mash half of the cooked potato and dice the rest for a variety of texture.

份量：12件
製作時間：45分鐘
To make: 12 pieces
Work Time: 45 minutes

蓮藕餅

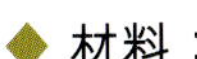

◆ 材料：

蓮藕8安士（225克），鯪魚肉4安士（100克），冬菇2隻，蝦米2湯匙，葱粒1湯匙，蛋黃1隻，麵粉1湯匙，鹽¼茶匙。

◆ 調味料：

鹽½茶匙，糖½茶匙，麻油、胡椒粉各少許。

◆ 製法：

1. 蓮藕去皮刨成長絲；冬菇及蝦米分別浸軟後切粒。
2. 魚肉與調味料拌勻，加入其餘材料拌勻，分成12等份。
3. 平底鑊燒熱，加油2湯匙，將蓮藕料逐份放入，用鑊鏟按平使成圓餅形，用中大火煎至兩面皆呈金黃色即可。

● 心得：

蓮藕須擦洗乾淨才去皮刨絲或切割，因中間空心處沾有之污泥是很難清除的。

◆ Ingredients:

8 oz (225g) lotus root
4 oz (100g) minced fish
2 pieces dried mushrooms
2 tablespoons dried shrimps
1 tablespoon diced spring onion
1 egg yolk
1 tablespoon plain flour
¼ teaspoon salt

◆ Seasonings:

½ teaspoon salt
½ teaspoon sugar
A little sesame oil
A little pepper

◆ Method:

1. Scrape lotus root to remove skin, grate into long shreds. Soak and dice mushrooms and dried shrimps separately.
2. Season minced fish, mix well with the rest of ingredients, divide into 12 equal portions.
3. Add 2 tablespoons oil in heated pan, spoon in each portion of lotus root mixture, press flat with fish slice to form a round patty, shallow-fry till golden brown on both sides. Finish all portions. Dish and serve.

● Practical Tip:

Scrub lotus root thoroughly before scraping, any dirty mud trapped in holes of lotus root is difficult to clean.

份量：16個
製作時間：30分鐘
To make: 16 pieces
Work Time: 30 minutes

韮菜粿

到食店中吃韮菜粿，有蒸的，也有煎的，但往往蒸的韮菜粿皮很厚，餡料不夠，煎的又往往嫌其太油膩。如果在家中自己動手，餡料份量可自行控制，若然採用煎的方法，煎好後還可細心用廚紙把油份吸乾，吃起來感覺會更好。

1.將粉料拌勻，用水開成軟粉糰
Mix all powdery ingredients with boiling water, mix to soft dough.

2.將小粉糰搓圓，捏成小碗狀，放入韮菜餡
Shape and knead dough as a small bowl, add fillings.

3.埋口，做成小圓餅形
Seal, roll and press flat to form green chives buns.

◆ 材料：

皮：粘米粉6安士（175克），澄麵粉1½安士（40克），糯米粉1½安士（40克），鹽少許，滾水1½杯，粘米粉3安士（75克）（後下）。

餡：韮菜10安士（275克），蝦米2湯匙，麻油1茶匙，鹽1茶匙，胡椒粉、糖各少許。

◆ 製法：

1. 粘米粉、澄麵粉及糯米粉篩勻，加鹽，沖入滾水，拌勻後撥入後下之粘米粉約3安士（75克），搓至不黏手及軟韌為合，平均分成16等份。
2. 韮菜洗淨，切粒；蝦米浸軟後切碎；將餡用材料混合拌勻醃15分鐘。最好用筲箕盛着，使去多餘水分。
3. 將每份粉糰搓圓捏成小碗形，包入適量韮菜餡，埋口略按成餅形，放入已塗油之碟或蒸籠內，大火蒸15分鐘。
4. 取出待冷，再用油煎至兩面呈金黃色，趁熱供吃。

● 心得：

1. 醃過的韮菜會溢出很多水分，如不瀝乾，放餡時皮會很易爆裂。
2. 後下之粘米粉是作薦手用的，可適量地搓入熱粉糰內。

◆ **Ingredients:**

Dough:
6 oz (175g) rice flour
1½ oz (40g) ungluten flour
1½ oz (40g) glutinous rice flour
Pinch of salt
1½ cups boiling water
3 oz (75g) rice flour, reserve

Filling:
10 oz (275g) green chives, diced
2 tablespoons dried shrimps
1 teaspoon sesame oil
1 teaspoon salt
A little pepper and sugar

◆ **Method:**

1. Sieve powdery ingredients, add a little salt, bind with boiling water. Mix well. Knead in reserved rice flour, approximately 3 oz (75g), to form a smooth and elastic dough.
2. Wash and dice green chives; soak and chop dried shrimps. Combine ingredients for filling, marinade for 15 minutes. Put in colander to drip excessive vegetable juice.
3. Shape each portion of dough into a round, knead to a bowl shape, add sufficient portion of filling, seal opening, press to the shape of bun, steam over high heat on a greased plate or a steamer for 15 minutes.
4. Cool and shallow-fry buns on both sides until golden brown. Serve hot.

● **Practical Tips:**

1. Seasoned chives tend to become watery. Filling should be drained before wrapping, if not, dough will crack easily.
2. The reserved rice flour is used for dredging. Knead in approximate amount to form soft dough.

份量：12個
製作時間：45分鐘
To make: 12 pieces
Work Time: 45 minutes

潮州粉粿

◆ **Ingredients:**

Dough:
6 oz (175g) ungluten flour
3 oz (75g) tapioca starch
Pinch of salt
1½ cups boiling water
3 oz (75g) tapioca starch, reserve

Filling:
6 oz (175g) pork
3 oz (75g) peanut
3 oz (75g) tapioca root
2 oz (50g) green chives
2 oz (50g) salted turnip

◆ **Seasonings:**
¼ teaspoon salt
¼ teaspoon sugar
1 teaspoon cornstarch
1 tablespoon water
½ tablespoon oil
A little pepper
A little sesame oil

◆ **Sauce:**
1 teaspoon cornstarch
½ teaspoon salt
½ teaspoon light soya sauce
2 oz (60ml) water
A little five-spice powder, reserved

◆ **Method:**
1. Sieve ungluten flour, tapioca starch and salt together. Pour in boiling water, mix well, cover for a while. Add reserved tapioca starch, mix to a smooth dough.
2. Dice and season the pork for 20 minutes. Deep-fry peanuts with skin on. Wash and dice tapioca root, green chives and salted turnip separately.
3. Cook pork in 1 tablespoon oil, add other ingredients, bind with sauce ingredients, remove from heat and sprinkle in five-spice powder, dish and cool.
4. Divide dough into 12 equal portions. Knead and press each to a round, wrap in sufficient filling, fold to form a half moon shape, shape to pleated Chiu Chow dumplings. Steam for 20 minutes over high heat.
5. Brush with cooked oil, serve hot.

● **Practical Tip:**
The tapioca starch specially for this transparent dough is available from shops that sell south-east Asian ingredients.

◆ **材料：**
皮：澄麵粉6安士(175克)，生粉3安士(75克)，鹽少許，滾水1½杯，生粉3安士(75克)(後下)。
餡：瘦肉6安士(175克)，花生3安士(75克)，沙葛3安士(75克)，韮菜2安士(50克)，菜角2安士(50克)。

◆ **調味料：**
鹽、糖各¼茶匙，粟粉1茶匙，水1湯匙，油½湯匙，胡椒粉、麻油各少許。

◆ **芡汁：**
粟粉1茶匙，鹽、生抽各½茶匙，水2安士(60毫升)，五香粉少許(後下)。

◆ **製法：**
1. 澄麵粉與生粉及鹽混合，用滾水沖熟拌勻，加蓋焗片刻，再撥入3安士生粉，搓至不黏手為合。
2. 瘦肉切粒後加調味醃20分鐘；花生連衣炸熟；沙角、韮菜及菜角洗淨後分別切粒。
3. 用1湯匙油起鑊加入肉粒炒熟，再加入其他餡料並埋芡，離火灑入五香粉取出待冷。
4. 將粉糰分成12等份，每份搓圓按扁，包入適量餡料，對摺成半月形，再打摺捏成粉粿形，大火蒸20分鐘。
5. 趁熱掃上少許熟油即可。

● **心得：**
如喜歡較韌之粉果皮，可往專門售東南亞用料之店舖買泰國生粉，也稱木薯粉，但一般家庭打芡用之生粉亦可。

TEA FLAVOURED EGGS

份量：12隻
製作時間：1小時
To make: 12 eggs
Work Time: 1 hour

茶  

◆ 材料：

雞蛋12隻，水3杯，八角4粒，桂皮1小片，茶葉(鐵觀音)2湯匙，片糖½斤(300克)，老抽½杯，生抽¼杯，鹽2茶匙。

◆ 製法：

1. 將蛋烚熟(約10分鐘)，敲裂蛋殼待用。
2. 將其餘材料煲滾，放入雞蛋，翻滾後收慢火煮15分鐘，熄火焗半小時。
3. 再將茶葉蛋煲滾，離火焗過夜。
4. 加熱後即可供吃。

● 心得：

茶葉汁料需以浸過蛋面為合。

◆ Ingredients:

12 eggs
3 cups water
4 stars aniseed
1 small piece cinnamon bark
2 tablespoons tea leaves (Tiguanyin)
½ catty (300g) slab sugar
½ cup dark soya sauce
¼ cup light soya sauce
2 teaspoons salt

◆ Method:

1. Hard-boil eggs for 10 minutes, crack shells.
2. Bring the rest of ingredients to boil. Add eggs, simmer for 15 minutes. Remove from heat, cover for ½ hour.
3. Re-boil tea-flavoured eggs and cover overnight.
4. Reheat and serve.

● Practical Tip:

All cracked eggs should be well covered by the tea-leaf sauce.

製作時間：1小時45分鐘

Work Time: 1 hour 45 minutes

鹵水牛腒

◆ **材料：**

牛腒1磅(450克)；薑1厚片，拍鬆；八角1粒；果皮1片；鹽¼茶匙；冰糖3安士(75克)；老抽½杯；生抽¼杯；玫瑰露酒1湯匙；水4杯。

◆ **製法：**

1. 牛腒洗淨出水後瀝乾；薑片拍鬆；果皮浸軟後去瓤。
2. 將水燒滾，加入所有材料，翻滾後收慢火炆1½小時。
3. 取出牛腒，稍凍後切片上碟。

● **心得：**

可用少許汁料埋少許生粉水煮滾淋於牛腒上，食味更佳。

◆ **Ingredients:**

1 lb. (450g) shin of beef
1 thick slice ginger
1 star aniseed
1 piece dried tangerine peel
¼ teaspoon salt
3 oz (75g) rock sugar
½ cup dark soya sauce
¼ cup light soya sauce
1 tablespoon Chinese Rose Wine
4 cups water

◆ **Method:**

1. Clean, blanch, rinse and drain shin of beef. Crush the ginger slice. Soak and scrape dried tangerine peel.
2. Boil water, add all ingredients, lower the heat when re-boils, simmer for 1½ hours.
3. Take out the sliced beef. Cool, slice and serve.

● **Practical Tip:**

For a juicier effect, thicken the remaining gravy with a little cornstarch solution and pour on the top of sliced beef.

製作時間：30分鐘

Work Time: 30 minutes

豬皮蘿蔔

豬皮、蘿蔔乃現今大行其道之“車仔麵”不可缺少的項目。此小食取食味之餘，豬皮之質感與佐膳之魚肚相似，亦是吸取膠質的好途徑，價錢亦較相宜。若能自行在家浸發，效果更佳。豬皮、蘿蔔俱為“索味”之材料，實為最佳配搭。

◆ 材料：

已發豬皮1磅（450克），白蘿蔔1磅（450克），薑2片，蒜肉2粒。

◆ 調味料：

水4杯，果皮1片，生抽半杯，老抽¼杯，糖1湯匙，鹽¼茶匙，麻油、胡椒粉各少許。

◆ 製法：

1. 將發好之豬皮切塊；薑片拍鬆；果皮浸軟，去瓤。
2. 白蘿蔔去皮，斜刀切角形，放滾水內大滾片刻使去苦澀味，過冷瀝乾。
3. 用2湯匙油爆香薑片及蒜肉，加白蘿蔔炒片刻，灒酒即加入調味料，煮滾，改用文火煮15分鐘。
4. 加入豬皮再煮15分鐘，離火焗至入味即可享用。

● 心得：

1. 浸發豬皮的方法：
   ①可往雜貨店或國貨公司的超級市場選購乾豬皮，用冷水浸1－2天至豬皮軟透。
   ②將浸透之豬皮原塊置大鍋滾水內焓至大滾，去除泡沫，可加薑葱使去腥味。
   ③將發好之豬皮置水喉下沖至凍透，搾乾水分，切塊即可使用。
2. 亦可在菜市場的豆腐檔中購買已浸發的豬皮。

◆ Ingredients:

1 lb. (450g) blanched pig's skin
1 lb. (450g) turnips
2 slices ginger
2 cloves garlic

◆ Seasonings:

4 cups water
1 piece dried tangerine peel
½ cup light soya sauce
¼ cup dark soya sauce
1 tablespoon sugar
¼ teaspoon salt
Dash of sesame oil and pepper

◆ Method:

1. Cut blanched pig's skin into irregular pieces. Crush the ginger slices. Soak the dried tangerine peel till soft and remove the pith.
2. Scrape turnips, cut into wedges, blanch, rinse and drain.
3. Sauté ginger and garlic on 2 tablespoons oil, add turnip, stir-fry for 1 minute, sizzle in wine and sauce, bring to boil, simmer for 15 minutes.
4. Add pig's skins, simmer for another 15 minutes, remove from heat. Keep covered to allow seasonings to soak through. Serve hot.

● Practical Tips:

1. To prepare home-made blanched pig's skin:
   ①This specially ingredient is in dry packet form and is available in most groceries or Chinese Emporium. Soak the dried pig's skin for about 24 hours until soft.
   ②Bring soften skin to a fast boil in a pot of boiling water with ginger slices and a stalk of spring onion.
   ③Drain, rinse under tap water, squeeze dry, trim and use.
2. Or, purchase blanched pig's skin from bean-curd shops in local wet market.

份量：12條
製作時間：45分鐘
To make: 12 rolls
Work Time: 45 minutes

齋 雞 扎

製作「齋雞扎」主要用的材料是腐皮和素雞，其實素雞也是用豆腐皮做的，大致是把腐皮放入以鹽、五香粉及醬油製成的調味汁中浸後捲成筒狀，用另一塊豆腐皮包好，用繩紮成螺旋形然後放水中煮熟而成。這一類的豆製品，都是很有營養而富蛋白質的食品，配上素餡料製成「齋雞扎」，食味和營養都未必比真的雞扎遜色呢！

1.將腐皮條放入滾油內炸鬆
Dip bean curd sheet in hot oil, lift immediately when bean curd sheet turns crispy.

2.撈起浸軟，即可捲食物用
Soak bean curd sheet in cold water, drain before use.

◆ 材料：

腐皮1塊，素雞2件，甘筍½個，西蘭花1個，冬菇4隻。

◆ 調味料：

鹽¼茶匙，糖¼茶匙，酒1茶匙，粟粉2茶匙，水4湯匙。

◆ 製法：

1. 腐皮抹淨，去硬邊，修剪成12條2"×6"(5厘米×15厘米)之長條。
2. 燒油一鑊至熱，將腐皮逐塊放入炸鬆，立刻撈起放入冷水中浸軟，取出瀝乾水分候用。
3. 素雞切成粗條，炸至金黃；甘筍切條出水；西蘭花切朵，用油鹽水灼熟；冬菇蒸熟，切條，用少許糖鹽油略醃。
4. 用1湯匙油將切條材料炒熱加入調味料，炒透盛起待冷。
5. 將浸軟之腐皮舖平，包上餡料，各款一條，捲起成雞紮狀；再將素雞紮置蒸籠內蒸8-10分鐘至熱即可。

● 心得：

如用雞肉、火腿、魚肚及冬菇作餡料，便成四寶雞紮。雞肉切條加調味醃好，魚肚用浸發豬皮的方法發好後切條，用少許調味料拌勻即可。

◆ Ingredients:

1 bean curd sheet
2 pieces vegetarian chicken
½ carrot
1 broccoli
4 Chinese mushrooms

◆ Seasonings:

¼ teaspoon salt
¼ teaspoon sugar
1 teaspoon Chinese wine
2 teaspoons cornstarch
4 tablespoons water

◆ Method:

1. Wipe bean curd sheet clean, trim into twelve strips in 2 inches x 6 inches (5cm x 15cm) strips.
2. Heat half wok of oil till very hot, add bean curd sheet piece by piece until puff up, lift and soften in cold water immediately, drain.
3. Cut vegetarian chicken in twelve thick strips. Deep-fry till golden brown. Cut carrot into twelve thick strips and blanch. Cut broccoli into twelve flowerlets and blanch in boiling water with a little oil and salt. Steam and cut Chinese mushrooms in strips, slightly season with sugar, salt and oil.
4. Stir-fry all ingredients with 1 tablespoon of oil till heated, add seasonings, stir well. Dish and cool.
5. On each bean curd sheet, roll in prepared filling accordingly. Arrange vegetarian chicken rolls on a Dim Sum plate and a bamboo steamer. Steam for 8-10 minutes, serve hot.

● Practical Tip:

For variations, use ham, seasoned chicken and blanched fish bladder (prepare as for blanched pig's skin), and Chinese mushroom as fillings.

VEGETARIAN PANCAKES

份量：6塊
製作時間：20分鐘
To make: 6 pieces
Work Time: 20 minutes

齋薄餅

◆ **材料：**

麵粉4安士(100克)，水6安士(200毫升)，甘筍絲、冬菇絲、齋火腿絲各1湯匙。

◆ **調味料：**

鹽½茶匙，糖¼茶匙，油1茶匙，胡椒粉、麻油各少許。

◆ **製法：**

1. 麵粉過篩，用適量清水開成薄漿，加入調味料及其他材料拌勻。
2. 燒熱平底鑊，加少許油，倒入適量粉漿料，用中火煎至底面呈金黃色即成。

● **心得：**

煎時稍用多點油便可做出脆皮薄餅；煎時用較少油，並將薄餅底面烙熟便可做出軟薄餅。

◆ **Ingredients:**

4 oz (100g) plain flour
6 oz (200ml) water
1 tablespoon each of shredded carrot, mushroom and vegetarian ham

◆ **Seasonings:**

½ teaspoon salt
¼ teaspoon sugar
1 teaspoon oil
Dash of pepper and sesame oil

◆ **Method:**

1. Sieve flour, mix in sufficient water to form a thin batter, add seasonings and shredded ingredients. Mix well.
2. Heat the frying pan, add 1 tablespoon oil and sufficient batter to cover the bottom of frying pan. Shallow-fry till golden brown on both sides. Dish and serve.

● **Practical Tip:**

Use less oil for soft pancakes and add 2 more tablespoons of oil to shallow-fry for a crispier result.

製作時間：30分鐘
Work Time: 30 minutes

齋鹵味

◆ **材料：**

炸麵筋10安士（275克），麻油½湯匙，麥芽糖1湯匙。

◆ **生粉水：**

生粉1茶匙與水1湯匙拌勻。

◆ **咖喱料：**

咖喱醬1滿匙（先用1湯匙落鑊爆香），素上湯1½杯，素食蠔油2湯匙，鹽½茶匙，糖½湯匙。

◆ **甜酸料：**

茄汁3湯匙，白醋3湯匙，素上湯1杯，糖2湯匙，鹽¼茶匙。

◆ **製法：**

1. 將炸麵筋炸硬，撈起瀝乾油分。
2. 鑊中留少許油，隨意將咖喱料或甜酸料加入，煮滾，放入炸過之麵筋，慢火煮至入味，約15－20分鐘。
3. 最後加入麻油及麥芽糖炒片刻，埋生粉水即可。

● **心得：**

購回來之炸麵筋雖已炸過，但必須再翻炸才炆煮，以免影響質感。若怕不清潔，可用吸油紙先吸去炸麵筋多餘的油分才使用，切勿用水洗，因落油較危險。

◆ **Ingredients:**

10 oz (275g) fried gluten
½ tablespoon sesame oil
1 tablespoon malt syrup

◆ **Cornstarch Solution:**

1 teaspoon cornstarch mix with 1 tablespoon water

◆ **Curry Sauce:**

1 level tablespoon curry paste (sauté in 1 tablespoon oil)
1½ cups vegetable stock
2 tablespoons vegetarian oyster sauce
½ teaspoon salt
½ tablespoon sugar

◆ **Sweet and Sour Sauce:**

3 tablespoons tomato ketchup
3 tablespoons rice vinegar
1 cup vegetable stock
2 tablespoons sugar
¼ teaspoon salt

◆ **Method:**

1. Deep-fry the fried gluten until firm, drain.
2. Heat curry sauce or sweet and sour sauce until boils, add fried gluten, simmer for about 15-20 minutes.
3. Add sesame oil and malt syrup, stir for a while, thicken with cornstarch solution, dish and serve.

● **Practical Tip:**

Deep-fry the fried gluten once more helps to keep the texture and shape after stewing. Do not rinse gluten, use kitchen paper to absorb excess grease for cleaning purpose.

BEAN CURD ROLLS IN OYSTER SAUCE

份量：12件
製作時間：30分鐘
To make: 12 pieces
Work Time: 30 minutes

鮮竹卷

街上吃到的鮮竹卷芡汁濃稠，一放涼了便結成啫喱狀，造型不很美觀。許多鮮竹卷的餡料又太少，皮太厚，吃下去口感也不佳。如果在家中自己動手，餡料方面可以「不惜工本」，製作時留意下芡汁的份量。如果製作得好，每令人有驚喜的感覺呢！

1.餡料放腐皮中央，包成春卷狀
Put filling on bean curd sheet, fold to the shape of a spring roll.

2.用少許餡料黏口
Use a little meat mixture to stick and seal edges.

3.將鮮竹卷炸鬆才炆煮至熟
Deep-fry bean curd rolls before putting to stew.

◆ **材料：**
鮮腐皮1張，免治枚頭豬肉10安士(275克)，蝦肉3安士(75克)。

◆ **調味料：**
鹽½茶匙，粟粉3茶匙，生抽¼茶匙，胡椒粉少許，麻油少許，水2湯匙。

◆ **芡汁：**
水¾杯，蠔油1湯匙，¼茶匙老抽，糖、胡椒粉、麻油各少許。

◆ **生粉水：**
生粉1茶匙與水1湯匙拌勻。

◆ **製法：**
1. 腐皮用濕布抹淨，去硬邊，修剪成12塊正方形，蓋好候用。蝦肉洗淨後切粒。
2. 將調味料拌勻，加入豬肉及蝦粒，拌至起膠，凍片刻，分成12份。
3. 腐皮放平，放入餡料，包成卷狀，用少許餡料封口，用中大火油炸至鮮竹卷鬆起，即可撈起。
4. 將芡煮滾，收慢火放入鮮竹卷炆15分鐘，埋生粉水，收汁後即可。

● **心得：**
可將炸好之鮮竹卷蒸熱及至軟身，將芡汁煮滾埋薄芡，淋在鮮竹卷上。

◆ **Ingredients:**
1 bean curd sheet
10 oz (275g) minced pork shoulder
3 oz (75g) shelled prawns

◆ **Seasonings:**
½ teaspoon salt
3 teaspoons cornstarch
¼ teaspoon light soya sauce
Shakes of pepper
Dash of sesame oil
2 tablespoons water

◆ **Sauce:**
¾ cup water
1 tablespoon oyster sauce
¼ teaspoon dark soya sauce
Pinch of sugar
Shakes of pepper
Dash of sesame oil

◆ **Thickening:**
1 teaspoon cornstarch
1 tablespoon water

◆ **Method:**
1. Wipe and trim bean curd sheet into 12 squares. Cover. Wash and dice the shelled prawns.
2. Season pork and diced prawns, stir well as a paste. Chill for a while. Divide into 12 portions.
3. Add a portion of filling on each bean curd sheet, wrap and seal with a little meat mixture. Deep-fry over medium-high heat until bean curd rolls puffs immediately. Drain.
4. Heat sauce ingredients, add bean curd rolls and stew over low heat for 15 minutes. Thicken, stir well.

● **Practical Tip:**
An alternate method is to steam the crispy bean curd rolls till cooked and become soft. Cook the sauce, thicken and pour on the top of bean curd rolls.

STEWED SPICY CHICKEN LEGS

製作時間：30分鐘

Work Time: 30 minutes

鹽水鳳爪

◆ **材料：**

鮮鳳爪1½磅(600克)，紹酒1湯匙，麻油1湯匙。

◆ **燉料：**

水3杯，果皮1小片，八角1粒，薑1厚片，鹽½湯匙。

◆ **製法：**

1. 鮮鳳爪洗淨剪去腳趾，出水瀝乾，置深鍋內。
2. 將燉料煲滾，慢火煮15分鐘至出味，離火加入紹酒拌勻，注入鳳爪中(以浸過鳳爪面為合)，大火燉2小時至稔，撈起置冰水內浸數小時。
3. 撈起鳳爪，掃上麻油即可，冷吃。

● **心得：**

亦可將燉好之鳳爪撈起熱吃，將沙薑粉拌少許麻油及熟油作蘸料同上桌。

◆ **Ingredients:**

1½ lb. (600g) chicken legs
1 tablespoon Shaoxing wine
1 tablespoon sesame oil

◆ **Seasonings:**

3 cups water
1 small piece dried tangerine peel
1 star aniseed
1 thick slice ginger
½ tablespoon salt

◆ **Method:**

1. Clean and remove claws from chicken legs, blanch, rinse, drain and put on a deep casserole.
2. Heat the ingredients for seasonings, simmer for 15 minutes, add Shaoxing wine and pour on top of chicken legs. Stew over high steam for two hours until tender. Drain and soak chicken legs in ice water for several hours.
3. Drain, brush with sesame oil. Serve cold.

● **Practical Tip:**

The chicken legs can also be served hot with a spicy sauce: prepare and mix spicy ground ginger powder with a little cooked oil and sesame oil.

製作時間：30分鐘
Work Time: 30 minutes

豉椒炒蜆

◆ 材料：

鮮蜆1½磅(600克)，蒜茸、豆豉茸、薑絲、紅椒絲各2湯匙，豆瓣醬1湯匙，酒1湯匙。

◆ 調味料：

蠔油1湯匙，鹽¼茶匙，糖1茶匙，生粉2茶匙，老抽1湯匙，胡椒粉、麻油各少許，水½杯。

◆ 製法：

1. 鮮蜆放清水內浸數小時使吐泥後瀝乾，放大鑊滾水內兜勻至開口即離火，置水喉下沖淨沙泥後瀝乾。
2. 用4湯匙油起鑊，爆香蒜茸、豆豉茸、薑絲及豆瓣醬，即下蜆炒勻，灒酒，加調味料，炒至汁收濃，加入紅椒絲，炒勻後上碟。

● 心得：

1. 經滾水煮過仍不開口的蜆即已死的蜆，需將之揀掉。用滾水煮至開口，再用蒜頭及辣椒煮過，既衛生又可口，可放心一試。
2. 炒蜆似乎是大牌檔壟斷之物，但現今人們怕貝類海鮮受污染，又怕食店煮得不衛生，因而雖是美味之物仍不大敢光顧。今天不妨在家大快朵耳。

◆ **Ingredients:**

1½ lb. (600g) fresh sea-water clams
2 tablespoons minced garlic
2 tablespoons crushed fermented black beans
2 tablespoons shredded ginger
2 tablespoons shredded chilli
1 tablespoon hot bean paste
1 tablespoon wine

◆ **Seasonings:**

1 tablespoon oyster sauce
¼ teaspoon salt
1 teaspoon sugar
2 teaspoons cornstarch
1 tablespoon dark soya sauce
A little white pepper
A little sesame oil
½ cup water

◆ **Method:**

1. Leave sea-water clams in water for several hours, drain and add to a large pot of boiling water, stir well over medium heat until open. Remove from heat, rinse under tap water, drain well.
2. Heat 4 tablespoons oil in wok, sauté garlic, fermented black beans, ginger and hot bean paste, add clams, stir well, sizzle in wine, add seasonings, stir until thickens, sprinkle in shredded chilli, dish and serve.

● **Practical Tips:**

1. Discard the unopened clams after blanching in boiling water. Pre-cooking clams in boiling water and stir-fry with garlic and chilli is a safe and palatable way of serving clams. Go ahead and have a try.
2. Quick-fried clams are supposed to be monopolised by the "Tai-pai-dong" (head-side food stalls), however, people are becoming more health-concious nowdays and tend to hesitate before eating out. Now you must enjoy this street-side clams at home.

STUFFED GREEN PEPPER

份量：12 件
To make: 12 pieces
製作時間：20 分鐘
Work Time: 20 minutes

釀青椒

◆ **材料：**

青椒3隻，剁爛或攪爛鯪魚肉8安士(225克)，冬菇1隻。

◆ **調味料：**

糖½茶匙，鹽¼茶匙，胡椒粉少許，生抽1茶匙。

◆ **製法：**

1. 青椒洗淨一開四，去籽；冬菇浸軟後切粒。
2. 鯪魚肉加調味料拌勻，攪至起膠，加入冬菇粒。
3. 將魚肉釀滿青椒件，掃平餡料，用中火油鑊，餡料向下煎至呈金黃色及魚肉變實即可。

● **心得：**

剁鯪魚肉時可逐少加入淡鹽水，使魚肉更易起膠及達彈牙效果。煎釀青椒時只煎魚肉一面，青椒那面不用煎，煎時經常轉動鑊子，效果更佳。

◆ **Ingredients:**

3 green peppers
8 oz (225g) minced fish
1 Chinese mushroom

◆ **Seasonings:**

½ teaspoon sugar
¼ teaspoon salt
Dash of pepper
1 teaspoon light soya sauce

◆ **Method:**

1. Cut green peppers into quarters and remove the seed. Soak and dice the Chinese mushroom.
2. Season minced fish, stir until firm and sticky, mix in diced mushroom.
3. Stuff green pepper with fish mixture, scrape surface smooth. Shallow-fry with the filling facing downward until golden brown. Drain and dish.

● **Practical Tip:**

When mincing fish, gradually sprinkle in salt solution to attain a sticky and crunchy result. Brown only the fish side, move pan occasionally when frying.

製作時間：30分鐘

Work Time: 30 minutes

釀茄子

◆ **材料：**

茄子（矮瓜）2條，蝦肉8安士(225克)，粟粉1湯匙。

◆ **調味料：**

鹽¼茶匙，粟粉½湯匙，胡椒粉少許。

◆ **製法：**

1. 茄子洗淨去蒂，斜刀切厚件。
2. 蝦肉用刀拍成蝦膠，加入調味料拌勻，置雪櫃內凍片刻。
3. 在茄子之一面切口沾上粟粉，掃上適量蝦膠，用刀掃平。
4. 鑊中燒油，用中上火放入釀茄子，蝦膠向下，半煎炸至蝦呈粉紅色，反轉再煎至茄子轉軟，即可上碟。

● **心得：**

煎茄子時，油要夠熱否則茄子易變黑，油分以浸過茄子一半及用高溫速煎法為宜。

◆ **Ingredients:**

2 egg plants

8 oz (225g) shelled prawns

1 tablespoon cornstarch

◆ **Seasonings:**

¼ teaspoon salt

½ tablespoon cornstarch

A dash of pepper

◆ **Method:**

1. Clean egg plants, remove stalks, cut at an angle into thick slices.
2. Mash shelled prawns, season and mix until sticky, chill for a while.
3. Dust one cut-side of egg plants with cornstarch, spread and stuff with shrimp paste.
4. Heat some oil, add stuffed egg plants with filling facing downward. Turn when cooked, slightly fry egg plants until soft. Drain and dish.

● **Practical Tip:**

Use medium-high heat when frying egg plants to avoid discolouring. Oil should be half way up to egg plants and cook with the "quick high-heat" method.

WORTIPS (MEAT DUMPLINGS)

份量：12個
製作時間：30分鐘
To make: 12 pieces
Work Time: 30 minutes

鍋貼

◆ **材料：**

麵粉5安士（150克），鹽少許，豬油½湯匙，暖水約½杯，免治腩肉8安士（225克），葱粒1湯匙，上湯1杯。

◆ **調味料：**

鹽½茶匙，糖½茶匙，生粉2茶匙，生抽2茶匙，酒½茶匙，胡椒粉、麻油各少許。

◆ **製法：**

1. 麵粉過篩，加鹽及豬油，用適量暖水開成一軟滑粉糰，放置一旁待約30分鐘。
2. 腩肉加調味料及葱粒，拌至起膠，置雪櫃內冷凍30分鐘。
3. 案板上灑粉，重搓粉糰，分成12小份，每份用木棍開成圓塊，包入適量餡料，一邊埋口，一邊打摺成鍋貼形。
4. 燒熱平底鑊，加油少許，放入鍋貼，注入上湯，加蓋文火煮約15分鐘至收汁。
5. 打開蓋，另加油1湯匙，煎至鍋貼底部呈金黃及鬆脆即可，熱食。

● **心得：**

將鍋貼餃打摺，需練習多次才成功。初做時，為免影響賣相，可用皮作餡，練習至合心水為止，重複多次，很快便可成為小師傅了！

◆ **Ingredients:**

5 oz (150g) plain flour
Pinch of salt
½ tablespoon lard
½ cup warm water
8 oz (225g) minced pork belly
1 tablespoon diced spring onion
1 cup chicken stock

◆ **Seasonings:**

½ teaspoon salt
½ teaspoon sugar
2 teaspoons tapioca starch
2 teaspoons light soya sauce
½ teaspoon Chinese wine
A little pepper and sesame oil

◆ **Method:**

1. Sieve plain flour, add salt and lard. Mix in sufficient warm water to form soft smooth dough, rest for 30 minutes.
2. Season minced pork, add diced spring onion, stir until sticky. Chill in the refrigerator for 30 minutes.
3. Knead and divide dough into 12 equal portions on a floured board. Roll each piece of dough to a round, wrap in a good lump of filling. Fold, seal and pleat to the shape of wortips.
4. Heat and grease a frying pan, add wortips and chicken stock, cover and cook for 15 minutes until cooked.
5. Open the lid, add 1 tablespoon oil, shallow-fry the bottom of wortips till golden brown and crispy. Serve hot.

● **Practical Tip:**

Shaping a pleated dumplings needs practice. For beginners, pinch a piece of dough for filling. Practice wrapping and pleating for several times and soon you will find yourself a professional dough chef!

份量：12串
製作時間：15分鐘
To make: 12 skewers
Work Time: 15 minutes

串燒沙爹牛肉

◆ 材料：
牛柳¾磅(300克)，麥芽糖1湯匙，凍開水1湯匙，竹籤12支。

◆ 調味料：
生抽½湯匙，粟粉1茶匙，糖1茶匙，葱頭茸1茶匙，胡椒粉少許，麻油少許，油2茶匙。

◆ 醬料：
沙爹醬2湯匙，咖喱粉½湯匙，胡椒粉½茶匙，糖1茶匙，老抽½湯匙，水2湯匙。

◆ 製法：
1. 將麥芽糖與1湯匙凍開水放碗內拌好，置熱水上座溶待用。
2. 牛柳切薄片，加調味料醃1小時，用竹籤串好置炭爐上燒至剛熟，淋上麥芽糖水再燒片刻。
3. 將醬料拌勻略煮與串燒牛肉同上。

● 心得：
雪藏牛肉較新鮮牛肉稔身。如用新鮮牛肉，可加少許鬆肉粉同醃。

◆ **Ingredients:**
¾ lb. (300g) beef fillet
1 tablespoon malt syrup
1 tablespoon water
12 skewers (or bamboo sticks)

◆ **Seasonings:**
½ tablespoon light soya sauce
1 teaspoon cornstarch
1 teaspoon sugar
1 teaspoon chopped shallot
Shakes of pepper
Dash of sesame oil
2 teaspoons oil

◆ **Sauce:**
2 tablespoons satay sauce
½ tablespoon curry powder
½ teaspoon pepper
1 teaspoon sugar
½ tablespoon dark soya sauce
2 tablespoons water

◆ **Method:**
1. Mix maltose syrup with 1 tablespoon water in a bowl and melt over a pot of hot water.
2. Slice and season beef fillet for 1 hour. Skewer in position. Roast beef on the charcoal stove until just done. Brush with malt syrup solution and roast for 1-2 more minutes.
3. Heat sauce ingredients. Serve with beef satay.

● **Practical Tip:**
Frozen beef is tenderer than fresh beef. If fresh beef is used, add a little meat tenderizer in the seasonings.

CHICKEN SATAY

份量：8串
製作時間：15分鐘
To make: 8 skewers
Work Time: 15 minutes

串燒沙爹雞肉

◆ **材料：**

雞肉8安士(225克)，竹籤8支。

◆ **調味料：**

生抽½湯匙，糖½湯匙，蒜茸1茶匙，胡椒粉少許。

◆ **沙爹醬：**

花生醬2湯匙，咖喱醬1湯匙，白醋1湯匙，黃糖1½湯匙，冷開水3湯匙，生抽1湯匙，老抽1湯匙。

◆ **製法：**

1. 雞肉切小片，加調味醃2小時，用竹籤串起。
2. 將網架掃油排上雞肉串，置炭爐上每面燒5分鐘至熟。
3. 將沙爹醬料拌勻略煮，與雞串同上。

● **心得：**

可用電烤爐代替炭爐，或置熱油內將雞串炸熟。

◆ **Ingredients:**

8 oz (225g) chicken meat
8 skewers (or bamboo sticks)

◆ **Seasonings:**

½ tablespoon light soya sauce
½ tablespoon sugar
1 teaspoon minced garlic
Shakes of pepper

◆ **Satay Sauce:**

2 tablespoons peanut butter
1 tablespoon curry sauce
1 tablespoon white vinegar
1½ tablespoons brown sugar
3 tablespoons water
1 tablespoon light soya sauce
1 tablespoon dark soya sauce

◆ **Method:**

1. Slice and season chicken meat for 2 hours. Skewer on bamboo sticks.
2. Arrange skewered chicken on a greased wire tack, roast on the charcoal stove on both sides until cooked.
3. Mix and heat ingredients for satay sauce, serve with roasted chicken.

● **Practical Tip:**

An electric grill can be used instead of a charcoal stove. Or, deep-fry chicken in hot oil.

常用材料

1. 糯米粉 Glutinous Rice Flour

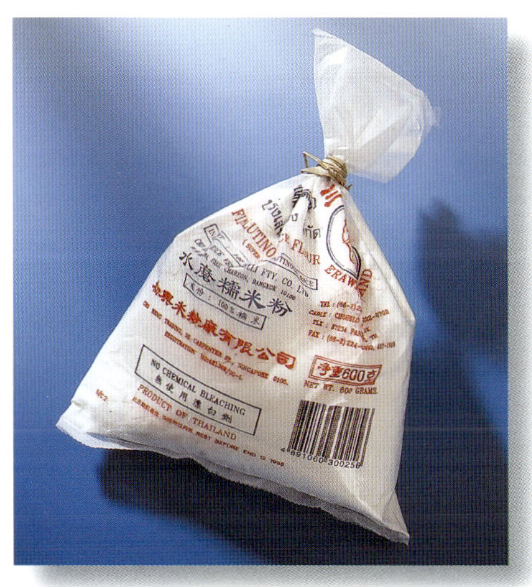

2. 粘米粉 Rice Flour

3. 自發粉 Self-raising Flour

4. 澄麵粉 Ungluten Flour

5. 西米 Sago

6. 花生 Peanut

7. 腐皮
Soya Bean Sheet

8. 八角
Aniseed

9. 豆沙
Red Bean Paste

10. 蓮蓉
Lotus Seed Paste

11. 麻蓉
Sesame Seed Paste

12. 麵粉
Plain Flour

常用工具

1. 迷你砵仔　Mini Clay Pots
2. 月餅模　Mould for Moon Cake
3. 水晶餅模　Mould for Crystal Cakes
4. 糖環模　Mould for Rosettes
5. 糖環模　Mould for Rosettes
6. 油掃　Brush
7. 木匙　Wooden Spoon

1. 隔篩　Sieve
2. 罩籬　Draining Ladle
3. 蘿蔔餅模　Mould for Turnip Cakes
4. 案板　Pastry Board
5. 木棍　Rolling Pin
6. 長竹筷　Long Bamboo Chopsticks
7. 撻模　Tart Moulds

1. 雞蛋仔模 Mould for Egg Puff
2. 量杯 Measuring Cup

常用單位換算表
Scale / Unit Conversion Table

為方便計算，下表各換算值均略經調整。

For convenience sake, the following conversion table has been rounded to the nearest whole number.

容量 (Volume)		
安士 (oz)	毫升 (ml)	杯 (cup)
1	30	⅛
2	60	¼
4	125	½
8	250	1
16	500 (1/2公升litre)	2
32	1000 (1公升litre)	4

重量 (Weight)			
安士 (oz)	克 (g)	両 (tael)	克 (g)
1	25	1	40
2	50	2	75
4	100	3	100
6	175	4	150
8	225	6	225
10	275	8	300
12	350	9	350
16 (1磅 lb.)	450	12	450
20	600	16 (1斤 catty)	600

註：為求統一，本書所列之材料均以安士及克為量度單位。為適應本地市場常用之斤／両及克，以達到製作的預期效果，讀者可參照上表作換算之用。

Remarks: The ingredient lists in this book are all scaled in terms of ounce and gram. To meet the popular use of catty / tael and gram in local markets and to achieve your masterpieces, readers are suggested to refer to the above tables for conversion.